AAT

Technician Level 4

Unit 10

Managing Accounting Systems

WORKBOOK

1159/J01

 FOULKS*lynch*

British Library Cataloguing-in-Publication Data

A catalogue record for this book is available from the British Library.

Published by Foulks Lynch Ltd
Number 4
The Griffin Centre
Staines Road
Feltham
Middlesex
TW14 0HS

ISBN 0 7483 5115 9

© Foulks Lynch Ltd, 2001

Printed and bound in Great Britain by Ashford Colour Press, Gosport, Hants.

Acknowledgements

We are grateful to the Association of Accounting Technicians, the Association of Chartered Certified Accountants, the Chartered Institute of Management Accountants and the Institute of Chartered Accountants in England and Wales for permission to reproduce past examination questions. The answers have been prepared by Foulks Lynch Ltd. The copyright to the questions remains with the examining body.

CONTENTS

		Page	
Preface – how to use this workbook		iv	
Case Study – Sealandair – Scenario		1	
		Questions	*Answers*
Working through the case study and your own organisation chapter by chapter		7	
Chapter 1	Report writing – not covered in the workbook		
Chapter 2	Organisation	9	14
Chapter 3	Systems and procedures	16	23
Chapter 4	Management and supervision	26	41
Chapter 5	Operational management	46	55
Chapter 6	Co-ordination	58	66
Chapter 7	Controls	69	74
Chapter 8	Training	76	83
Chapter 9	Improving the system	86	93
Chapters 10 – 12	Control systems in practice	95	109
Chapter 13	Fraud management	111	116
Case study – Sealandair – final report		119	
Additional scenarios and reports		127	

PREFACE – HOW TO USE THIS WORKBOOK

This is the 2001 edition of the AAT workbook for the Revised Standards of Unit 10 – Managing Accounting Systems.

This workbook differs from all the other workbooks that Foulks Lynch publishes because Unit 10 is assessed in a unique way – namely by use of a 4,000 word project.

The textbook has covered all the theory and practical techniques you need when assessing the effectiveness of an accounting system and the ways in which it can be improved. What this workbook now does is to lead you through a practical way you can put this into practice in preparation for writing your project. The workbook does this in two ways:

1   THE CASE STUDY SEALANDAIR

1.1   The scenario

On page 1 of this workbook you will find the case study Sealandair. The scenario on which this case study is based lays out the workings of a small travel agency, with sufficient detail to enable you to gain an appreciation of its organisational structures and also some detail of its accounting systems.

1.2   Chapter by chapter analysis

Each chapter of the workbook is cross-referenced to the same chapter number in the textbook. The workbook chapters highlight the key issues that the textbook chapter raises and leads you through how you might assess Sealandair's performance in those various areas. It does this by means of a series of 'lead questions', the answers to which are structured by a series of standard findings based on SWOT analysis (Strengths, Weaknesses, Opportunities, Threats). (Note that this is not a rigorous application of SWOT analysis which usually makes a very firm distinction between the internal and the external environment. Here we do rather merge the two environments in order to produce a simpler more practical solution to the requirements of this project.)

The questions of a typical key area, illustrated below are taken from the first question of Chapter 2 – we do not cover Chapter 1 of the textbook in this way because that deals with report writing.

Key areas, illustrated below, are:

---

1   Activity - Centralisation and decentralisation

Are the degrees of centralisation and decentralisation appropriate?

Leads:

Are you able to make your own decisions about how you approach your work?
Is your opinion requested by your senior managers, respecting your local knowledge?
Would you or your colleagues like to have more attention paid to your thoughts and ideas?
Do you sometimes feel that decisions taken centrally show a lack of understanding of what you actually do?

Findings
Strengths
Weaknesses
Opportunities
Threats
Action
Responsibility
Priority

When you are working through the case study Sealandair, you should not actually write your findings etc onto the page of the workbook itself. You should use these pages when you are performing the case study on your own organisation as described in paragraph 2 below. Rather, you should make neat notes of the relevant findings in relation to Sealandair and then compare them to the suggested findings at the end of the chapter.

1.3   Suggested answer to case study lead questions

At the end of each chapter, we provide suggested answers to the case study lead questions. These are brief and highlight the key findings. They may also include material not strictly in the scenario. We have tried to keep the scenario brief – the answers occasionally employ a little imagination of what one would typically find.

---

1   Solution – Centralisation and decentralisation

Findings – We stand alone as we are not part of a chain with a head office. Apathy leads to us all being able to do our own thing to a large extent. Sometimes it is good, because we can apply our own knowledge unhindered. However, some staff would like more coordination, as we sometimes end up pleasing ourselves rather than considering colleagues and customers.

Strengths – We can work unhindered; some centralisation would be welcome.

Weaknesses – Our internal decentralisation is unplanned.

Opportunities – To coordinate our working practices.

Threats – The apathy in the firm.

Action – Heads of sections to plan out integrated working practices between sections.

Responsibility – Heads of sections

Priority – High.

1.4   Sealandair – final report

At the end of the book, starting on page 119, you will find the final report of Sealandair, which may represent something of a model for the report you may wish to produce for your own organisation.

2   WRITING THE REPORT ON YOUR OWN ORGANISATION

2.1   Introduction

Having worked through the case study Sealandair, you are now in a position to assess the effectiveness of your own organisation's systems and write the final report.

The steps you should take mirror exactly the steps you have just worked through with the case study Sealandair.

2.2   Work through the activities in each chapter

As with Sealandair, you should consider each activity in each chapter and report your findings using the SWOT analysis method. Your findings should be kept fairly brief unless there is something of major significance. Remember that the findings that we have provided for the Sealandair case study are only guides to the sorts of considerations you should be making, and your own organisation will naturally differ from these.

Note the important point (which is occasionally referred to in the Sealandair case study) that you may not always be able to get the information that you are seeking. Some systems simply may not exist; other systems may exist but you may not be in a position to gain full information about them.

2.3   Writing your final report

You will now be in a position to write the final report on your own organisation. You may follow any structures you choose for this report; our structure is:

(a)   summary of findings
(b)   recommended for action
(c)   conclusion.

You could present the conclusion first if you wished as a sort of 'executive summary'.

Remember that the balance of your report may differ from the Sealandair report. You may wish to become more involved in the actual internal controls and workings of the accounts department itself, and perhaps concentrate less on the leadership and motivational aspects. That is absolutely fine but do remember that balance is the key word here; a report that concentrates exclusively on one or two major areas to the exclusion of all others will not be balanced and the assessment of such report may reflect this.

CASE STUDY –

SEALANDAIR

SCENARIO

1   SEALANDAIR – THE BACKGROUND

Sealandair is a travel agency, situated in the High Street of a small but affluent town. The business was established in 1976, by a former tour rep, Connor Turisst, who is approaching retirement. Mr Turisst is on the premises each day – though he needn't be – from 10 in the morning until 5 at night; but he makes no secret of his desire to sell up and retire by 60. Of course, the more efficient the business, the more profitable it will become, and the better the selling price it will command. Mr Turisst therefore wants increased efficiency.

The agency has a total of 14 staff, including Mr Turisst. Four staff look after the accounts, including the section leader James Berry, whose work we see in the activities at the end of each chapter of the workbook. There is one secretary, three foreign exchange clerks, and five sales staff. Each section has a section leader, collectively known as the senior staff.

None of the staff – except Mr Turisst – can really say they love their work, but neither do they especially hate it. The rates of pay are nothing special, the offices and their equipment are rather shabby, business is quite brisk but not as much as you would think considering the location, and the computer equipment in each area is rather dated. The staff are generally lacking in dynamism, though James is trying to 'escape' to a real accounting firm via the achievement of an AAT qualification. As such there is little enthusiasm, or chance of promotion in the firm. The last person to join did so 9 years ago when her predecessor left.

Mr Turisst likes change, but only if it is the type that can be paid into the bank. If he is making money then he is happy; potential never came into it... until now of course, and the thought of selling the business for a good sum. However he faces a dilemma..... if he does spend money on improving the look of the business, will he get it back when he sells it? Perhaps not.... no, it's efficiency from the staff that is the best option for him.

Although this is a travel business, the accounting system is at the very heart of it. Whether it be in the sale of tickets, the costing out of special offer bargain trips, or the exchange of foreign currency, the accounting staff are involved. As such, the efficiency of the accounts staff impacts directly on that of all other staff.

You can assume that James has permission to focus his report on the accounting department in which he works, and that all agency staff are willing to cooperate, to alleviate boredom as much as anything. Mr Turisst is very keen to see the report on completion..... increased efficiency, you will recall, is his chosen way to a higher sale value for the business.

2   SEALANDAIR – MORE DETAIL ON ORGANISATIONAL MATTERS

(a)   **Organisational structure**

Sealandair operates without reference to environmental factors. There is little competition in the town where the business is based.

As the firm is not part of a chain, there is not a significant centralisation-decentralisation question to address.

There is no organisation chart.

The firm is run on informal lines, so this informality is unplanned and arises from managerial apathy.

Staff are organised into specialist sections, facilitating expertise in their operations, however the facility does not assist to cross cover roles, which sometimes results in the need to employ expensive external temporary staff.

The staff appreciate the need to learn about the procedures involved in their own work, but essentially carry on their business in the same way as they always have done.

(b)   **Information technology and organisational structure**

The computer systems are dated, but serve procedural needs.

The relationship between benefits and costs cannot be determined, as the firm's cost structure cannot be determined.

Budgeting is used as a control method, operating via a standard costing system with variance analysis.

(c)   **Management: nature, style and motivation**

Senior staff believe they are effective as managers to a certain degree, because they have been running the business for many years. They do appreciate that improvements could be made.

Senior staff feel they have power over junior staff. They see their acts of delegation as being too free time for higher duties, but junior staff see delegation as work dumping.

The staff are motivated in numerous ways. Increased pay is popular, but not as a serious motivation element.

There is no personnel department in this small firm, but staff feel they are treated in a humane way; not as a resource.

Individual objectives are not set.

(d)   **Teamwork**

There are formal planned groups, for example the accounts team. Social groupings exist, for example at lunch time.

Communication is not seen as a process, and so is not planned. Feedback is not regularly given to confirm understanding.

There is much time wasted in the firm, without any realisation of the cost which attaches.

(e)   **Accounting problems**

Fraudsters had sent invoices to several thousand companies. These requested payment for an entry in a trade directory.

The directory did not, however, exist. Sealandair was one of the companies which had paid the £2,000 charge.

Sealandair's accounting system was recently computerised. All invoices are keyed straight into a standard accounting package. The company's accounting department is short staffed and so the default settings on the package have been set to minimise the amount of clerical effort required to process transactions. If, for example, an invoice is received from a new supplier, the program will automatically allocate an account number and open an account in the purchase ledger. At the end of every month, the program calculates the amount which is due to each creditor; a cheque for each creditor is automatically printed out for the total of all of the invoices from that creditor input during the month. When the system was first installed, the accountant used to review creditors' accounts prior to the cheque run as a check that the system was not being abused. This review was, however, discontinued because of pressure of work and because there were too many invoices to review properly.

3   SEALANDAIR - METHODOLOGY

James' notes and report are included in the work book, but these are very much his own, relating to his accounting system and not yours. No two people's reports will ever be exactly the same as long as human judgement is involved, even when based on the very same accounting system at the very same time in the firm's life.

Gain value by looking at HOW James approached the report in the context of Sealandair that you have just read, thinking seriously about WHY he draws his conclusions and makes his decisions. However, I hope you will be critical as I explain further below. Every course of action you recommend must be supported by the evidence you obtain; objectively, impartially and credibly serving the context of your firm's operations and the stated purpose of the report. Context + evidence + wisdom (theory) = decision.

You will find that the firm is stagnant to the point of irritation, and has little scope for improvement within its resource constraints, the general apathy that prevails, and the fact that the firm is due to be sold – and therefore changed – quite soon. In short, a very difficult decision to resolve.

Even James, who feels he is dynamic, has stagnated, and you will see that in what he writes. You are not like that of course, and so you will cast a critical eye over James' findings for each activity, saying to yourself..... 'Is this really the best he can say? Could he not get nearer to the heart of the matter? Is he giving up before he starts?'

James' report is good, but again ask yourself if it could be better? More incisive? More informative? More critical? More creative? More dynamic? And a very important aspect indeed..... does the report arise directly from the findings, or does he add in his own opinions? The report you write must link directly to what you have found, and not to what you would have liked to have found.

You need to learn to pass this critical eye over things, because that is what your tutor will do with you and your work! It is easier to take the critical route over someone else's (ie, James') work because you look at it with fresh eyes; with your own work you get in too deep, and can't always see the wood for the trees.

The activity thus trains you to think one level higher than the average report writer, so your tutor has less chance of knocking your work back. It demands that you **think** rather than just read, an approach that should be employed in every academic subject you approach. So go on..... beat that tutor!

WORKING THROUGH THE CASE STUDY AND YOUR OWN ORGANISATION

Chapter 2

ORGANISATION

1 ACTIVITY – CENTRALISATION AND DECENTRALISATION

Are the degrees of centralisation and decentralisation appropriate?

Leads:

Are you able to make your own decisions about how you approach your work?
Is your opinion requested by your senior managers, respecting your local knowledge?
Would you or your colleagues like to have more attention paid to your thoughts and ideas?
Do you sometimes feel that decisions taken centrally show a lack of understanding of what you actually do?

Findings

Strengths

Weaknesses

Opportunities

Threats

Action

Responsibility

Priority

2   Activity – Organisation charts

Do organisation charts exist, and are they used to any effect?

Leads:

Ask your managers to show you the firm's organisation chart if you have not already seen it, and provided one exists.

If an organisation chart does not exist, why do you think this is?
Should one be drawn up, and for what reasons?

How can the existence of an organisation chart help you to work more efficiently within your accounting system?

Who would use the organisation chart?

Findings

Strengths

Weaknesses

Opportunities

Threats

Action

Responsibility

Priority

3   Activity – Symptoms and consequences of structural deficiency

Do you sometimes feel your organisation is 'falling apart'?

Leads:

Are colleagues over-burdened?
Do you find yourself surprised by sudden changes in strategy?
Do you feel your organisation does not know where it is going?
Are there frequent criticisms that the management do not know what they are doing?

Findings

Strengths

Weaknesses

Opportunities

Threats

Action

Responsibility

Priority

4   Activity – Specialisation

Specialists are seen as experts, but is that what your firm really needs?

Leads:

Are those that specialise in one specific area always well motivated and efficient?
Could they get bored doing the same thing every day?
What would happen if a specialist became ill; would there be someone to take his place?

Findings

Strengths

Weaknesses

Opportunities

Threats

Action

Responsibility

Priority

5   Activity – Power, authority and delegation

Do you and your colleagues really understand these terms?

Leads:

Does a hunter have power over its prey?
Do you perceive yourself as having any power?
Why should people want power?
Why might you describe your managers as having authority?
Is work ever 'dumped' on you in the name of delegation?
Are you personally accountable, or is your role accountable?
Who is responsible for what happens in your accounting system?

Findings

Strengths

Weaknesses

Opportunities

Threats

Action

Responsibility

Priority

1   Solution – Centralisation and decentralisation

Findings – We stand alone as we are not part of a chain with a head office. Apathy leads to us all being able to do our own thing to a large extent. Sometimes it is good, because we can apply our own knowledge unhindered. However, some staff would like more coordination, as we sometimes end up pleasing ourselves rather than considering colleagues and customers.

Strengths – We can work unhindered; some centralisation would be welcome.

Weaknesses – Our internal decentralisation is unplanned.

Opportunities – To coordinate our working practices.

Threats – The apathy in the firm.

Action – Heads of sections to plan out integrated working practices between sections.

Responsibility – Heads of sections.

Priority – High.

2   Solution – Organisation charts

Findings – We are a very small business, and we know who we are, what we do and our relationships to each other.   All are clear whom they should report to.

Strengths – We are achieving the goals of an organisation chart without the need of a chart.

Weaknesses – None of significance.

Opportunities – To draw up a chart, though this seems futile.

Threats – None apparent.

Action – not required.

Responsibility – Not applicable.

Priority – Not applicable.

3   Solution – Symptoms and consequences of structural deficiency

Findings – A basic structure exists: the boss, and the senior staff. Also in terms of function: counter sales; accounts staff etc. We all seem to manage quite well, but continued success depends on the environment remaining stable. We are to be sold quite soon, perhaps to a chain where our way of working would not be appropriate, and the changes demanded difficult for staff to face.

Strengths – The structure, although basic, works for us quite well.

Weaknesses – It depends on the co-operation of the staff, a very undependable state of affairs. Any change could throw it in to complete disarray and demotivate staff.

Opportunities – To formalise and clarify the structure, after confirmation it is correct for us.

Threats – From future lack of co-operation, and the demands of a new owner.

Action - Clarify the structure.

Responsibility – Mr Turisst.

Priority – Low in the most short term.

4 Solution – Specialisation

Findings – We are already specialised by section, but there are problems with covering the senior staff when they get ill. We always find it hard to cope. We go into panic when the one secretary is not here, as the boss resists paying for expensive admin-agency secretaries. Staff are happy to remain as sales staff or accounts people etc.

Strengths – Specialisation means we have expertise in our own fields.

Weaknesses – Insufficient training for effective cover to be given when senior staff are absent, and when the secretary goes off. The cost of secretaries brought in is very high.

Opportunities – Training to motivate staff, vary their working life and provide a feeling of motivation and progression in an environment where promotion is non-existent unless staff leave (rare).

Threats – Cost of brought in staff; poor service internally and externally when trying to cover absent senior staff.

Action – Training programmes to be implemented.

Responsibility – Senior staff

Priority – High.

5 Solution – Power, authority and delegation

Findings – senior staff feel that have some power over junior staff. They see delegation as necessary to free time for higher duties. Junior staff see delegation as work dumping. No significance of abuse of power.

Strengths – no abuse of power

Weaknesses – perception of work-dumping which demotivates

Opportunities – to use delegation effectively and to motivate

Threats – loss of co-operation from staff who feel they are being used

Action – application of correct delegation procedures

Responsibility – senior staff

Priority – medium

Chapter 3

SYSTEMS AND PROCEDURES

1   Activity – The nature and function of organisational structure

Is your firm geared up structurally for optimum performance during periods of change, some of which could be fast moving, and/or painful?

Leads:

Do you think the structures in your firm are adequate?
What would you have to do to bring about structural changes?
What resources would be required and how would you justify their use?

Findings

Strengths

Weaknesses

Opportunities

Threats

Action

Responsibility

Priority

2   Activity – Systems approach in an organisation structure context

Does your firm, through its activities, add value to any existing resource it uses?
Is your accounting system subject to influences from within the firm?
Is your firm subject to influences from outside?
Are you ever able to work without any reference to external influences?
If you are subject to external influences, how should you manage your interaction with them?
Through your activities, are there examples of value you add, and are they measurable?

Findings

Strengths

Weaknesses

Opportunities

Threats

Action

Responsibility

Priority

3   Activity – Development v growth

Do you know which to focus upon?

Leads:

How many colleagues understand the difference between development and growth?
Should they know the difference between the two? Why?
Do these concepts apply to your accounting system?
Which if any is more important in respect of: a) the short term; b) the long term?

Findings

Strengths

Weaknesses

Opportunities

Threats

Action

Responsibility

Priority

4   Activity – Information

Is information technology at the heart of your firm's structure?

Leads:

Can your colleagues explain the difference between data and information?
How can you change data into information?
What are the qualities of good information?
Why is good information needed?

Findings

Strengths

Weaknesses

Opportunities

Threats

Action

Responsibility

Priority

◆ FOULKS*lynch*

5   Activity – Information: benefit/cost

Is the information you obtain worth the cost?

Leads:

How can you determine the true cost to your accounting system of information you use, bearing in mind that you will probably be sharing it with other areas of the firm?
Who in the firm records and accounts for the cost of information?
Is the estimation of cost accurate?
How can information costs be reduced?

Findings

Strengths

Weaknesses

Opportunities

Threats

Action

Responsibility

Priority

6   Activity – Information and organisations

Is information just information? Can you ever have too much?

Leads:

Ask your managers what information needs they have.
Ask the same question of your colleagues.
Consider the dangers of having too little or too much information.
Are your information systems computerised? If not, should they be?

Findings

Strengths

Weaknesses

Opportunities

Threats

Action

Responsibility

Priority

7   Activity – The systems view of an organisation

How are the firms sub-systems grouped into a major system?

Leads:

Identify the sub-systems within existing systems.
Are the groupings of sub-systems logical?
Are the goals of one sub-system compatible with the goals of other sub-systems?
Do the staff working within sub-systems appreciate that they are doing this?

Findings

Strengths

Weaknesses

Opportunities

Threats

Action

Responsibility

Priority

1   Solution – The nature and function of organisational structure

Findings – We are a very small business and rather individual. Should we become part of a chain structures would be more applicable, but then these should already exist in the corporate structure we would become part of, ready for imposition on to what would become our 'branch'.

Strengths – The structure appears to work.

Weaknesses – It could not stand change, and change is on the horizon.

Opportunities – To gear ourselves up for change in advance, to minimise the culture shock we could face.

Threats – A rapidly imposed changed structure on sale of the business. The demotivation could have an adverse effect on our effectiveness.

Action – Discuss possible changes and how we can deal with them.

Responsibility – The staff; Mr Turisst is not going to be here post sale.

Priority – Medium at present.

2   Solution – Systems approach in an organisation structure context

Findings – We just haven't thought about this.

Strengths – If we haven't planned this, there is sure to be areas for improvement and efficiency gains.

Weaknesses – We do not have much time to devote daily to such a large task.

Opportunities – Efficiency gains, as yet unquantified.

Threats – We may be subject to down-sizing & staff redundancies if taken over.

Action – Gain knowledge of systems theory and plan changes. Get to understand the existing system (we may not know it exists, but it is sure to in some form).

Responsibility – Senior staff in consultation with all staff.

Priority – High.

3   Solution – Development v growth

Findings – Vague understanding of the terms and their interaction.

Strengths – None.

Weaknesses – Lack of understanding.

Opportunities – To learn and capitalise on a planned approach to the benefits of both, and the relationship of strategies related to each.

Threats – Apathy from a lack of understanding of the importance of the terms and their relationship.

Action – Educate all staff, and discuss significance and management implications.

Responsibility – Me, at first as I am studying this, but then senior staff.

Priority – High.

4   Solution – Introduction

Findings – Our computer systems are dated, but we do get the information we need in terms of procedural work. Note, however, the lack of an accounting information system.

Strengths – Procedural information is good

Weaknesses – Management information is not good

Opportunities – To improve management information

Threats – Business failure from a lack of management information; cost of IT systems

Action – Improve information through IT application

Responsibility – Mr Turisst and senior staff

Priority – Medium

5   Solution – Information: benefit/cost

Findings – Where information is lacking, we have little idea of the relationship between benefit and cost.

Strengths – A lot of the information appears to be produced cheaply, but internal costing. Does not take place in a methodical manner.

Weaknesses – Lack of knowledge of benefits and costs.

Opportunities – More justification for an effective accounting information system.

Threats – Losing the benefit of information, or obtaining information which costs more than it earns us.

Action – Integrate with accounting information system implication.

Responsibility – Mr Turisst and senior staff.

Priority – Based on present limited knowledge, a medium priority is advised.

6   Solution – Information and organisations

Findings – We don't feel we generate too much information internally. We know we are lacking in management information... but what exactly?

Strengths – Internal generation not excessive.

Weaknesses – Not knowing what we need.

Opportunities – Start establishing and planning information needs.

Threats – Danger of missing out on the benefits of good information.

Action – Plan information needs.

Responsibility – Senior staff.

Priority – Medium.

7   Solution – The systems view of an organisation

Nothing to add at this stage – can't get the information. Note to student; this might happen several times. You cannot expect to get an answer to everything, but you should know how to deal with the situation arising. How? Well use it as the basis of a recommendation for action within your firm.

Chapter 4

MANAGEMENT AND SUPERVISION

1   Activity – Key interests

Do individuals' key interests ever conflict with the requirements of the firm?

Leads:

Can you readily identify the key interests of individuals?
Do you have evidence that these interests have been placed above corporate interests?
Can you identify any areas of actual or potential conflict?
Why should such a conflict be significant?

Findings

Strengths

Weaknesses

Opportunities

Threats

Action

Responsibility

Priority

2   Activity – Decision-making and problem-solving

How complex and risky can this be?

Leads:

What is the difference between the two terms?
Are all of your colleagues good decision-makers? Are you?
Is anyone apparently afraid of decision-making? What impact would that have on the firm?
Will there be just one solution?
Can we forget the problem once a solution is found?

Findings

Strengths

Weaknesses

Opportunities

Threats

Action

Responsibility

Priority

3   Activity – Major strategies for organisational control

How well is your firm controlled by its managers?

Leads:

Look at the types of control featured in the text book, and see if any apply to your firm.
Can you suggest a better one than that currently in existence?
Who chooses the control strategies in your firm?
To what extent is your accounting system controlled?
How successfully?
How do you measure success?

Findings

Strengths

Weaknesses

Opportunities

Threats

Action

Responsibility

Priority

4   Activity – Supervisory control strategies

Are controls applied to activities compatible with those applied to people?

Leads:

Do your colleagues complain of overly restrictive control put on them?
Is the task perceived by colleagues to be more important than themselves?
Is there a way you can control staff and activities harmoniously?

Findings

Strengths

Weaknesses

Opportunities

Threats

Action

Responsibility

Priority

5   Activity – The effective manager

Can we ever claim to be effective managers?

Leads:

Identify what an effective manager should do in the firm.
Compare this to the way your managers manage.
Can you reasonably expect any manager to be totally effective?
Where do we draw the line between accepting managers' failings and condemning them?

Findings

Strengths

Weaknesses

Opportunities

Threats

Action

Responsibility

Priority

6   Activity – Management style and employee behaviour

Should managers adopt one style for life?

Leads:

Identify the different management styles of your managers.
Does the style vary in different situations?
Does the style vary with different individuals or groups?
Are you ever consulted about decisions affecting your accounting system?
Do your managers treat you as a person or a resource?
How do you and your colleagues react to different management styles?
Are you happy in your work?
Do you feel valued?

Findings

Strengths

Weaknesses

Opportunities

Threats

Action

Responsibility

Priority

7   Activity – Motivation in theory and practice

Are we all motivated by the same things?

Leads:

Are you made to perform, or encouraged to perform?
Are you motivated by the same things as your colleagues?
Does Maslow's 'Hierarchy of Needs' apply to you?
Are you still 'excited' by your last pay rise?
How do you expect to be rewarded for extra effort, if at all?
Could a PRP scheme be applied to your accounting system?

Findings

Strengths

Weaknesses

Opportunities

Threats

Action

Responsibility

Priority

8   Activity – Management in the future

Are we cutting too deep?

Leads

Is your accounting system designed to cope with all kinds of changes?
Could the cost of extra staff be justified by a better service provision?
How effective is the upward and downward communication between superiors and subordinates?
Do subordinates assist in planning how to put senior management strategies into action?
Do you think some staff are focusing on personal ambitions rather than what is best for your firm?
Could your firm benefit from having less layers of management?
Is your accounting system fast and responsive within a fast and responsive firm?

Findings

Strengths

Weaknesses

Opportunities

Threats

Action

Responsibility

Priority

9   Activity – Organisational objectives and individual objectives

Why should we try to match these objectives?

Leads:

Do you and your colleagues believe in your firm's objectives?
If not, what can and should be done about it?
What are the objectives of your accounting system?
Does achieving them motivate you in any way? Should it?

Findings

Strengths

Weaknesses

Opportunities

Threats

Action

Responsibility

Priority

10   Activity – Leadership and management style

Is there a link between the two?

Leads:

What is the difference between management and leadership?
Are some of your best managers poor leaders or vice versa?
How easy is it to be a good manager and a good leader?

Findings

Strengths

Weaknesses

Opportunities

Threats

Action

Responsibility

Priority

11   Activity – Decision-making in organisations

How far can you go?

Leads:

Do you feel comfortable asking for help with problems?
Is participation a normal part of your firm's decision-making?
Are you certain of your personal level of authority?
Can you admit you got it wrong without losing face?

Findings

Strengths

Weaknesses

Opportunities

Threats

Action

Responsibility

Priority

12   Activity – Creating an effective work team

Should group members have specific roles?

Leads:

Do you notice group members adopting specific roles?
Are some group members better suited for some roles than others?
Have you noticed inefficiency where group members are very alike?
Do groups need a leader? Should this role be planned or natural?
What happens to the effectiveness of a group when one or more members 'step out of line'?

Findings

Strengths

Weaknesses

Opportunities

Threats

Action

Responsibility

Priority

13   Activity – The nature and importance of good communications

Is it good to just talk?

Leads

Do you know for sure what formal communication channels exist?
Are you able to give feedback to management, or are you merely spoken at?
Can you tell the difference between rumour and informal communication?

Findings

Strengths

Weaknesses

Opportunities

Threats

Action

Responsibility

Priority

14   Activity – Methods of communication

Should you use all methods available to you?

Leads:

How many channels exist in your firm?
Are they all appropriate to every situation?
Can you think of areas for improvement?
How easy is it to communicate your project ideas?

Findings

Strengths

Weaknesses

Opportunities

Threats

Action

Responsibility

Priority

15   Activity – The concept of excellence

Is it enough for individuals to be excellent at what they do?

Leads:

What does excellence mean to you?
What evidence of commitment to excellence can you find in your firm?
Are you and your colleagues in need of greater corporate excellence?

Findings

Strengths

Weaknesses

Opportunities

Threats

Action

Responsibility

Priority

1   Solution – Key interests

Findings – There is much evidence of staff protecting their own daily requirements, at the cost of efficiency.

Strengths – We are small enough to communicate displeasure to each other effectively.

Weaknesses – Demotivating. Bad for efficiency. Hard to get a judgement.

Opportunities – Chance to formalise procedures, and make decisions based on efficiency of the firm rather than the desires of the individual.

Threats – From demotivation through inter-section rows, and inefficiency.

Action – Establish an ethos of putting the firm and its customers first.

Responsibility – Senior staff.

Priority – High.

2   Solution – Decision-making and problem – solving

Findings – We are good at making the decisions required to solve the problems, considering the primitive nature of our systems. There are too many problems due to lack of planning.

Strengths – Good at using what we have.

Weaknesses – We do not have much, and lack of planning makes things worse.

Opportunities – More justification for information systems and planning.

Threats – Decisions unnecessarily poor and problems more frequent than necessary.

Action – Integrate needs here with other related areas already covered.

Responsibility – senior staff.

Priority – High.

3   Solution – Major strategies for organisational control

Findings – Mr Turisst leaves us alone for the most part. The senior staff give out instructions to their staff but the system is not formal.

Strengths – We are not over controlled, and it is motivating to be able to make your own decisions.

Weaknesses – Sometimes people take advantage – taking long lunch hours for example, or trying to buck the dual control system.

Opportunities – Coordinating control strategy, so that how you behave is in the firm's interest and not that of certain individuals.

Threats – We could drift in to a very weak state - frauds could occur - our reputation could suffer.

Activity – Implement a formal management control system.

Responsibility – Mr Turisst and senior staff.

Priority – Low.

4   Solution – Supervisory control strategies

As per task 1.

5   Solution – The effective manager

Findings – We can claim to be effective to a certain degree, if for no better reason than that we have been operating the business for many years. However, there are many improvements that are possible, or so it seems, if we all tried to grasp the management techniques that professional researchers have developed.

Strengths – We have some effectiveness, and know that more is possible.

Weaknesses – We manage in a rather unstructured way.

Opportunities – To grasp techniques which are proven to lead to greater effectiveness.

Threats – From apathy, and a refusal to see the benefit has been higher than the cost.

Action – Develop a general ethos in the organisation of trying to learn about and introduce new management techniques.

Responsibility – All staff. Some will not be managing, but those being managed should have an input.

Priority – High.

6   Solution – Management style and employee behaviour

Findings – Even in our small firm we see many different styles coming through, depending on the importance of the task, who is executing it, and under what circumstances. Some people have styles which are appreciated more than others. All staff agreed that managers must manage, but they also said they worked better for managers that appreciated them. However, those people managing seemed to have a different view of their management style and its effectiveness to those being managed by them.

Strengths – A wide variation of management styles to suit different conditions.

Weaknesses – The styles do not always work.

Opportunities – To take a fresh look at how we interact with each other.

Threats – Some staff members feel their style of management is better than those been managed feel it is.

Action – To have meeting groups to discuss why styles are used and how they are received.

Responsibility – Senior staff.

Priority – Medium.

7   **Solution – Motivation in theory and practice**

Findings – We are motivated by different things; no one thing can be applied to all of us. However, we all agree we would like more pay. Pressing for lasting motivation the general consensus was for a happy working atmosphere, job security and fair treatment from senior staff. Mr Turisst said he wanted to just get out with a good pay off, and was looking forward to retiring to his villa in Greece.

Strengths – The general consensus is that job security is important and is obtained.

Weaknesses – The status quo will change most probably when the new owners take over.

Opportunities – We can aim to treat each other well at least.

Threats – Demotivating action from the new owners.

Action – Continue to treat each other well, as we do, but to try that bit harder.

Responsibility – All of us.

Priority – Low, because we treat each other quite well already.

8   **Solution – Management in the future**

Findings – we are not in the position of many people we know working in other firms. The harsh management techniques and conditions that prevail elsewhere have largely been avoided in our small and rather old-fashioned firm. We do not want to undergo radical change unless we have been a part of the decision-making process.

Strengths – Our present set-up works.

Weaknesses – We are very old-fashioned and could work to a more modern and efficient plan.

Opportunities – To bring ourselves more up to date.

Threats – From how we would react to changes from the new owner if radical. We could be very demotivated if change was swift and forceful.

Action – Prepare ourselves for a possible rapid up-dating of how we operate.

Responsibility – All of us.

Priority – Medium.

9   **Solution – Organisational objectives and individual objectives**

Findings – Not really any stated objectives, except work hard and make the business money. We go along with this. We don't really push each other around; we just get on with it.

No further comment

10   **Solution – Leadership and management style**

Findings – Our managers are good to work for, but there is not one that appears to be a leader taking us off to new areas of activity, or guiding us toward improved working practices.

Strengths – We like working with senior staff.

Weaknesses – We lack direction.

Opportunities – To give the business some direction, change and growth.

Threats – We could drift in to a non-viable state.

Action – Senior staff to act dynamically and creatively, and lead us on to new areas and practices.

Responsibility – Mr Turisst and staff.

Priority – High.

11   Solution – Decision-making in organisations

Findings – We just get on with our jobs; we know how far we can go, and when to seek a higher authority.

Strengths – The approach works for us.

Weaknesses – Difficult for new members of staff to join in, though new members are rare.

Opportunities – Codify authority and responsibility.

Threats – None identified.

Action – Codify responsibility and authority.

Responsibility – Senior staff.

Priority – Low.

12   Solution – Creating an effective work team

Findings – We have our own designated jobs to do, know what they are, and get on with them so we are effective in that sense; however we could be missing out on better practices.

Strengths – We are effective teams.

Weaknesses – We could be missing out on better practices.

Opportunities – To acquire the better practices.

Threats – Losses due to not optimising efficiency.

Action – Apply group theory to our groups.

Responsibility – Me, as I am studying this on my course.

Priority – Medium.

13   Solution – The nature and importance of good communications

Findings – We do a lot of talking, but not so much listening. The communication ratio does not apply, this being..... we have two ears and one mouth, and they should be used in those proportions.

Strengths – We do talk.

Weaknesses – We do not listen.

Opportunities – To build on our talk, adding listening, to turn it into communication.

Threats – Important ideas could be missed.

Action – We should learn to listen more, and feedback our understanding to confirm we have actually understood what is being said to us.

Responsibility – All of us.

Priority – High.

14   Solution – Methods of communication

Findings – We do not have a great range of methods to communicate, as we are a very small set up. Basically our system is one of memos, notes stuck to chairs and face to face chats; very unstructured. It would be more efficient if we could communicate on screen with each other, to avoid wasting time walking round to each other's desks.

Strengths – The low range of methods suits the firm.

Weaknesses – Time wasted in walking from office to office.

Opportunities – To use internal e-mail to save unnecessary walks which often leave a customer unattended to.

Threats – The cost of time wasted and the displeasure of customers who are in a hurry.

Action – Introduce internal e-mail.

Responsibility – To be justified to Mr Turisst by senior staff, and then to be ordered by Mr Turisst.

Priority – Medium.

15   Solution – The concept of excellence

Findings – We do not talk of excellence; we just want to do a good job.

Strengths – We are actually trying for excellence in our own small ways.

Weaknesses – We could be doing much more.

Opportunities – To change our approach.

Threats – Lost quality of service.

Action – Discuss the concept.

Responsibility – Senior staff.

Priority – Medium.

Chapter 5

OPERATIONAL MANAGEMENT

1   Activity – Evaluating efficiency and effectiveness

Do you really appreciate the meaning and significance of efficiency and effectiveness, and how could you measure each one?

Leads:

Ask your colleagues what they understand by the terms efficiency and effectiveness.
As both are intangible, how would you measure them?
Should your accounting system be efficient and effective?
Can a system be efficient and effective if the rest of the firm is not?

Findings

Strengths

Weaknesses

Opportunities

Threats

Action

Responsibility

Priority

2   Activity – The learning organisation

Is your firm continually transforming through on-going learning?

Leads:

When things go wrong, are they usually blamed on 'circumstances beyond control'?
Do such errors continue to arise?
Is there evidence that your firm tries to learn from its mistakes and plan to avoid them?
Is there a firm-wide ethos of the progression of the business, and the individual, through continual learning (corporate and personal experience)?

Findings

Strengths

Weaknesses

Opportunities

Threats

Action

Responsibility

Priority

3   Activity – Developing strategy

What is strategy?

Leads:

Ask your managers about their views on what strategy means.
Think about how and why strategies are created?
Why is strategic planning usually in the hands of the senior managers?
How will planning affect your accounting system?

Findings

Strengths

Weaknesses

Opportunities

Threats

Action

Responsibility

Priority

4 Activity – Contingency planning

Does your firm plan ahead to minimise problems, or try and solve them as they arise?

Leads:

How would you know if contingency plans exist?
How can you tell if they are sufficient?
What are the costs and benefits of contingency planning?
What are the costs and disadvantages of not planning for contingencies?
Does contingency planning take place at all levels, or just at senior levels?

Findings

Strengths

Weaknesses

Opportunities

Threats

Action

Responsibility

Priority

5   Activity – Introduction

Is time money?

Leads:

Do you expect to be paid for your time at work?

Findings

Strengths

Weaknesses

Opportunities

Threats

Action

Responsibility

Priority

6   Activity – The significance of time management

How much time can you waste in a day?

Leads:

Does a minute lost here or there matter?
Are you happy to lose a pound here or a pound there?
If you account for money, should you not account for time?
How much does wasted time cost?

Findings

Strengths

Weaknesses

Opportunities

Threats

Action

Responsibility

Priority

7   Activity – Daily scenes in a poorly time-managed accounting office

Do you rule time or does it rule you?

Leads:

Do you often run out of time?
Are you prone to leaving work half–finished?
Do you plan your diary ahead of time?

Findings

Strengths

Weaknesses

Opportunities

Threats

Action

Responsibility

Priority

8   Activity – Time leaks

How many ways can you find to waste time?

Leads:

In what ways do your colleagues waste time?
In what ways do you think you waste time?
Do you and your colleagues really know how much time you are wasting and how?

Findings

Strengths

Weaknesses

Opportunities

Threats

Action

Responsibility

Priority

◈ **FOULKS***lynch*

9   Activity – Effective techniques for improving time management

Can we really improve the way we manage time?

Leads:

Have you or your colleagues any time-saving ideas that work?
What is the cost of the time you have wasted today?
Does your accounting system operate a system of prioritising work?
Could you benefit from the use of planning aids?
Do you review the progress of your day?
Are you in a position to delegate? If yes, then what?

Findings

Strengths

Weaknesses

Opportunities

Threats

Action

Responsibility

Priority

1   Solution – Evaluating efficiency and effectiveness

Findings – We understand the meaning of efficiency and effectiveness, but we don't know if we have it.

Strengths – Knowing what the terms mean.

Weaknesses – Not knowing our efficiency and effectiveness levels.

Opportunities – To find gaps in our efficiency and effectiveness and find ways to bridge them.

Threats – Lost profit; lost jobs.

Action – Once an accounting information system is installed, we must learn how to interpret it.

Responsibility – Mr Turisst and senior staff.

Priority – High after an accounting information system has been installed.

2   Solution – The learning organisation

Findings – We learn as individuals in terms of procedures we execute, but as a firm we carry on much the same despite problems met successfully or unsuccessfully.

Strengths – Procedural learning.

Weaknesses – Lack of learning by the firm.

Opportunities – To establish a learning approach.

Threats – From repeating costly mistakes.

Action – Educate all staff, and discuss significance and management implications.

Responsibility – Me, at first as I am studying this, but then senior staff.

Priority – High.

3   Solution – Developing strategy

Findings – We don't have one, except for Mr Turisst wanting to make money.

Strengths – None.

Weaknesses – We are very vulnerable.

Opportunities – To establish agreed, planned definitive strategy.

Threats – Who is going to want to buy our shaky set-up?

Action – Formulate strategy.

Responsibility – Mr Turisst and senior staff.

Priority – High.

4   Solution – Contingency planning

Findings – Individuals contingency plan sometimes, but we normally solve problems as they arise.

Strengths – Staff appreciate the process if not always the name.

Weaknesses – We are allowing problems to arise when we could plan to avoid them.

Opportunities – To save ourselves the time and cost of problem solving.

Threats – Loss of business through poor customer service, and higher than necessary costs.

Action – Formulate and formalise contingency plans.

Responsibility – Senior staff.

Priority – High.

5   Solution – Introduction

Note to student – This was included to set the scene, so no findings etc are required.

6   Solution – The significance of time management

Findings – Lots of evidence of time wasting.

Strengths – We are beginning to appreciate the cost.

Weaknesses – We have not fully worked out the cost.

Opportunities – To cost it out.

Threats – Time wasting eats into our profits.

Action – Time study.

Responsibility – Senior staff.

Priority – High.

7   Solution – Daily scenes in a poorly time-managed accounting office

Findings – Lack of planning of time; frequent problems meeting schedules.

Strengths – None.

Weaknesses – We blame our problems on anyone or anything except ourselves.

Opportunities – To learn how to manage time.

Threats – Inability of staff to see they have a problem.

Action – Time management courses.

Responsibility – Senior staff to arrange; Mr Turisst to approve.

Priority – High.

8   Solution – Time leaks

Findings – Staff were amazed to see how many leaks there were in the firm, once they knew what to look for.

Strengths – Staff now see the leaks.

Weaknesses – We have got a lot to learn about filling them.

Opportunities – To learn.

Threats – From apathy regarding plugging the leaks.

Action – Time management courses.

Responsibility – Senior staff to arrange; Mr Turisst to approve.

Priority – High.

9   Solution – Effective techniques for improving time management

Findings – We hardly know any.

Strengths – None.

Weaknesses – Lack of technique.

Opportunities – To learn techniques.

Threats – Apathy.

Action – Time management courses.

Responsibility – Senior staff to arrange; Mr Turisst to approve.

Priority – High.

Chapter 6
CO-ORDINATION

1   Activity – Informal organisations

Is the balance between informality and formality suitable to maximise effectiveness?

Leads:

Is your work environment well-structured or very easy going?
Do you ever feel too constrained or not constrained enough?

Findings

Strengths

Weaknesses

Opportunities

Threats

Action

Responsibility

Priority

2   Activity – The systems approach to problems

How are activities co-ordinated together for success and value addition?

Leads:

Can any staff or managers identify any formal systems within the firm?
Is there evidence that they are working effectively – e.g. optimum co-ordination and value addition?
How does your accounting system fit into, or interface with, other systems in the firm?
Do you feel that your firm's systems work effectively together?
If there are no systems in existence, what is your firm missing?
Can systems be readily designed and implemented?

Findings

Strengths

Weaknesses

Opportunities

Threats

Action

Responsibility

Priority

3   Activity – General features of groups

Is a group merely a collection of people?

Leads:

How many different kinds of group can you identify in your firm?
How differently do they behave in different situations?
Are these formal or informal groups?
Are some people members of several groups?
Do individuals behave differently in different groups?
Does your accounting system make up one or several groups?
Are there different methods required to manage different groups?

Findings

Strengths

Weaknesses

Opportunities

Threats

Action

Responsibility

Priority

4   Activity – Methods of influence

How do you get colleagues to do what you want?

Leads:

Should you use one method all the time?
Have your managers ever pushed you too far?
Do you react best to 'carrots' or 'sticks'?
Can you influence by force?
If you are made to do something, does it mean you have been influenced?

Findings

Strengths

Weaknesses

Opportunities

Threats

Action

Responsibility

Priority

5   Activity – Organisational conflict

What is the significance of conflict?

Leads:

Can conflict be productive as well as destructive?
How do you manage groups where members conflict?
Have you seen group members try to 'hijack' groups for their own interests?
How should conflict be resolved? By expelling group members?

Findings

Strengths

Weaknesses

Opportunities

Threats

Action

Responsibility

Priority

6   Activity – Conflict between work groups

Do we all work for the same firm?

Leads:

Have you experienced competition between groups within your firm?
Why do you think this happens?
In a highly competitive world, should internal competition be allowed by firms?
Is there a way of focusing different groups on the same goals?
Should the strength of a particular group be allowed to let it win in the contest for resources?
Do strong managers in your firm control inter-group conflict?

Findings

Strengths

Weaknesses

Opportunities

Threats

Action

Responsibility

Priority

7   Activity – Stress

Is stress all bad?

Leads:

Do you feel stressed? If yes, what exactly do you mean?
If no, are you missing something?
Have you noticed that stress can be productive as well as destructive?
Do you find a managed level of stress is good for performance?
Can stress be used as an excuse for poor performance?
How do you manage stress when some originates from outside your firm e.g., at home?

Findings

Strengths

Weaknesses

Opportunities

Threats

Action

Responsibility

Priority

8   Activity – The role of the accountant

An add-on or an essential part?

Leads:

How well does your accounting system integrate with non-financial activities, such as 'marketing'?
How does your accounting system assist the non-accountants?
How do the non-accountants help you?
Do you share any 'common ground' with non-accountants?
Are other departments customers of yours?
Should you be providing a service to colleagues as you would to customers?

Findings

Strengths

Weaknesses

Opportunities

Threats

Action

Responsibility

Priority

1   Solution – Informal organisations

Findings – We are very informal, although occasionally Mr Turisst comes up with what he feels is a great idea, and we have to implement it. The informality is unplanned, and arises from apathy. Sometimes it is frustrating, because there is no way to force colleagues to cooperate. However, we do all get on with each other in the main.

Strengths – We have known each other for a long time and can handle the informality. The small size of our business is appropriate for such informality.

Weaknesses – Informality arising from apathy rather than planning.

Opportunities – To formalise the informality by laying down a code to show how formality can be substituted when required.

Threats – We may start to fall apart if apathy increases. There could be quite a culture shock if we are taken over by a chain.

Action – Discuss the need for occasional formality.

Responsibility – All staff, lead by senior staff.

Priority – Low.

2   Solution – The systems approach to problems

Findings – When we coordinate for success it is because we feel it is good working practice, but no systems assessment exists. No value addition discussion takes place.

Strengths – Evidence of coordination for success.

Weaknesses – Unplanned; no value addition by design.

Opportunities – to plan a successful system.

Threats – not sure at this point as I am not sure how much or little systems activity takes place.   Certainly it is not by dedicated planning.

Action – Gain knowledge of systems theory and plan changes. Get to understand the existing system (we may not know it exists, but it is sure to in some form).

Responsibility – Senior staff in consultation with all staff.

Priority – High.

3   Solution – General features of groups

Findings – We have our own groups, e.g. the accounts team, and these are planned and formal. However, lunch time trips to, say, the pub take place in cross-functional groups, e.g. three staff from ticketing and one from accounts always meeting for lunch on an informal basis. Gossip and rumour often come out of these groups. The staff act differently in these informal groups to when they are in their functional groups.

Strengths – Mixing of staff humanises the firm.

Weaknesses – It is practically impossible to manage the informal groups, and prevent their gossip.

Opportunities – Use some of these cross -function groups in brain-storming sessions, to learn how best to serve each other.

Threats – The destructive force of gossip, and general activity which is unmanaged.

Action – Use good communication to kill of the need for gossip.

Responsibility – Senior staff.

Priority – Medium.

4   Solution – Methods of influence

Findings – We all know where we stand and so accept requests from each other. Resistance to work-dumping.

Strengths – Acceptance of requests.

Weaknesses – Resistance.

Opportunities – To remove resistance.

Threats – Loss of efficiency via lack of cooperation.

Action – All staff to examine how they get things done through people.

Responsibility – All staff.

Priority – High.

5   Solution – Organisational conflict

Findings – There are some rows between staff, but it was felt they serve to clear the air. We know each other too well to fall out seriously.

Strengths – Constructive aspect to conflict.

Weaknesses – Nothing significant.

Opportunities – Exploit positive side to conflict.

Threats – Allowing conflict to get out of hand to destructive levels.

Action – Ensure conflict does not become destructive.

Responsibility – All staff.

Priority – Low.

6   Solution – conflict between work groups

Findings – Different areas of the firm have different priorities, and there is antagonism between, say, ticket sales staff and the lone secretary who may be behind in sending out tickets.

Strengths – The conflict pushes us to give a good internal service, if for no other reason than to avoid giving another section a chance to complain.

Weaknesses – Lack of understanding of each other's circumstances.

Opportunities – Understand each other's problems more.

Threats –The splitting of the firm into rival factions.

Action – Keep groups on the same side.

Responsibility – Senior staff.

Priority – Medium.

7   Solution – Stress

The replies to this were flippant and of no use to the project

Note to student – you cannot guarantee a sensible answer. If the answer is not sensible, you just have to leave it out of your research. Do not press people too much if they are in a silly mood, because you will lose their cooperation in the long-term.

8   Solution – The role of the accountant

Findings – Once comments over rivalry were passed, all accounting staff did appreciate the service aspect of their role, and their own needs to receive service from other sections.

Strengths – Professional attitude.

Weaknesses – None.

Opportunities – To develop an already good attitude by discussion with other sections of their service requirements and ours.

Threats – The possibility that we may feel we have already achieved all we need to.

Action – Arrange a plan for development.

Responsibility – Me.

Priority – Medium.

Chapter 7

CONTROLS

1 Activity – The data processing system

What constitutes a data processing system?

Leads:

Look into different kinds of processing system.
Consider those provided by external companies.
How would the design of the processing system assist your firm to be efficient?

Findings

Strengths

Weaknesses

Opportunities

Threats

Action

Responsibility

Priority

2   Activity – Budgets as a tool for control

What kind of budgets exist?

Leads:

Find out from your senior staff which budgets are used, if you are not already involved.
What is the point of budgeting?
Who is assisted by the use of budgeting techniques?
To what degree are budget variances, negative or positive, acceptable?

Findings

Strengths

Weaknesses

Opportunities

Threats

Action

Responsibility

Priority

3   Activity – Quality–related costs

Is quality control worth the cost?

Leads:

What is the cost of quality control?
What is the cost of not controlling quality?

Findings

Strengths

Weaknesses

Opportunities

Threats

Action

Responsibility

Priority

4 Activity – Total quality management

Are you continually trying to improve quality?

Leads:

Is there much talk of quality in your firm?
How can you improve quality in your accounting system?
Does your firm have a staff member responsible for quality?
Do you have pride in the service you provide?
Are relationships built with your customers?
Do you measure your success and discuss the results?

Findings

Strengths

Weaknesses

Opportunities

Threats

Action

Responsibility

Priority

5   Activity – Team briefings and quality circles

Is your accounting system worth special and specific attention?

Leads:

Do some communications relate specifically to your systems?
Should your team have full opportunity to discuss team matters?
Has your team specific messages management needs to hear?

Findings

Strengths

Weaknesses

Opportunities

Threats

Action

Responsibility

Priority

1   Solution – The data processing system

Findings – We need help.

Strengths – We know we need help.

Weaknesses – We are not sure where to get it or if we can afford it.

Opportunities –To bring in professionalism from outside.

Threats – It could be too costly.

Action – Consult professional consultants, but after we have given the matter much thought.

Responsibility – Senior staff in consultation with all staff.

Priority – High.

2   Solution – Budgets as a tool for control

Findings – We operate a standard budget system with variance analysis.

Strengths – It works quite well.

Weaknesses – It has not been upgraded for 10 years.

Opportunities – Greater financial control.

Threats– Problems from insufficient information.

Action – Investigate new methods (computer based in our case).

Responsibility – Me.

Priority – Medium.

3   Solution – Quality related costs

Findings – Couldn't get any response here.

Strengths – None.

Weaknesses – No information.

Opportunities – Cannot exploit any yet.

Threats – What are we missing?

Action – Investigate the concept.

Responsibility – Me.

Priority – Low (investigation may change this priority).

4   Task 6 – Total quality management

Findings – We do not have formal quality systems in place, but many customers come back to us year after year, and we do like to do the best we can for our customers.

Strengths – We give a good service according to the remarks of many of our customers.

Weaknesses –It is unstructured, and left to the goodwill of the staff as long as that exists.

Opportunities – To think about how we could improve our service quality.

Threats – We could end up spending more time writing about quality than delivering it.

Actions – Keep up the good service but try and make it always that bit better.

Responsibilities – All of us, but led by senior staff.

Priority – Medium.

5   Solution – Team briefings and quality circles

Findings – Nobody knew what a quality circle was. We have quite a few briefings.

Strengths – The briefings work well.

Weaknesses – We do not have quality circles.

Opportunities – The benefit from forming quality circles.

Threats – Our service (to customers and ourselves) could be lacking in quality.

Action – Set up a quality circle.

Responsibility – Senior staff.

Priority – Medium.

Chapter 8
TRAINING

1   Activity – Organisation development

Does your firm follow up its learning with the process of developing?

Leads:

Are there plans for managing change?
Are members of staff being retrained?
Can you see evidence of policies co-ordinated across the firm?
Would your colleagues understand the term 'change agent'?
Are you being consulted on development of your own accounting system?

Findings

Strengths

Weaknesses

Opportunities

Threats

Action

Responsibility

Priority

2 Activity – Skills needed for implementation of strategy

Do you have the necessary skills in your organisation?

Leads:

You will need to ask senior management what experience they have in crafting strategy.
How can you tell if the skill level available is sufficient?
Should local knowledge be included from staff lower down in the hierarchy?

Findings

Strengths

Weaknesses

Opportunities

Threats

Action

Responsibility

Priority

3   Activity – The nature of human resource management

Are we humans, resources or both?

Leads:

Is personnel management only the work of personnel managers?
What does your personnel department do for you?
Could it do more?
Is there any link between personnel management and the service you provide?

Findings

Strengths

Weaknesses

Opportunities

Threats

Action

Responsibility

Priority

4 Activity – Assessing human resource needs

Should we just cut staff to the minimum to minimise costs?

Leads:

Does your accounting system have the right kind of staff?
Could you need different staff to cope with future changes?
What skills might be needed?
If two staff resigned, how would you maintain a good service?

Findings

Strengths

Weaknesses

Opportunities

Threats

Action

Responsibility

Priority

5   Activity – Human resource development

Should we have recruited staff in the first place if they needed developing?

Leads:

What does development mean?
Is training a part of development or vice versa?
How has your accounting system developed in the last year?
What staff development is needed to keep up?
How can you contribute to the development process?
[Is this project part of your development?]

Findings

Strengths

Weaknesses

Opportunities

Threats

Action

Responsibility

Priority

6   Activity – Appraisal

Is appraisal enough on its own?

Leads:

What happened at your last appraisal?
What decisions/plans arose out of the appraisal?
Were they enacted and followed up?
Do you fear appraisal or welcome its assistance?
Is appraisal a formal or informal process in your firm? What should it be?

Findings

Strengths

Weaknesses

Opportunities

Threats

Action

Responsibility

Priority

7   Activity – Development of business professionals

Are there jobs in your firm or careers?

Leads:

Does everyone want a career?
Is your accounting system a stepping stone in anyone's career path?
How do you maintain service continuity if people are continually moving on?
Do 'job' staff feel inferior to 'career' staff? Would they tell you?

Findings

Strengths

Weaknesses

Opportunities

Threats

Action

Responsibility

Priority

1   Solution – Organisation development

Findings – There has not been much change to manage.

Strengths – None.

Weaknesses – Falling way behind the times, and not being able to handle change.

Opportunities – Keeping up to date; finding effective change-management policies which are sure to be needed in the future.

Threats – We could end up a commercial dinosaur in an environment we couldn't handle.

Action – Strategic planning.

Responsibility – Mr Turisst and senior staff.

Priority – High.

2   Solution – Skills need for implementation of strategy

Findings – Sorely lacking in experience.

Strengths – Some experience from other employments (senior staff).

Weaknesses – Our ignorance.

Opportunities – Training.

Threats – Costs may cause training to be abandoned.

Action – Assess skills gaps and methods and costs of bridging them.

Responsibility – Senior staff.

Priority – High.

3   Solution – The nature of human resource management

Findings – We do not have a personnel department; we are too small. We are treated in a humane way, and not as a resource.

Strengths – We are treated well.

Weaknesses – We may not fit in to a chain of agencies if taken over by one.

Opportunities – Try and persuade Mr Turisst to persuade the new owners to carry on treating us well.

Threats – Having to adapt to the personnel and resource management approach of a large agency chain, if that is who we are taken over by.

Actions – Persuade Mr Turisst.

Responsibility – Senior staff.

Priority – Medium.

4   Solution – Assessing human resource needs

Findings – We have a good range of experience, and sufficient numbers for our small premises. The problem arises when the secretary goes off sick.

Strengths – Staffing levels (except secretary); experience.

Weaknesses – Only one secretary.

Opportunities – None on the horizon.

Threats – If the secretary is out we have problems getting tickets etc delivered on time, which could be very bad for business.

Action – Think of ways of covering the secretary.

Responsibility – Senior staff.

Priority – High.

5   Solution – Human resource development

Findings – The staff are not sure if they need developing for the most part..... they wonder if there are new computer links they could work on with the major airlines and tour companies, or more efficient ways of ticketing.

Strengths – None.

Weaknesses – Not knowing what to develop into.

Opportunities – Develop into more efficient working methods.

Threats – If there are computerised methods and the airlines etc choose to abandon the older methods of dealing with them, we could be in trouble.

Actions – Liase with our major companies.

Responsibility – Senior staff.

Priority – Medium.

6   Solution – Appraisal

Findings – The senior staff have a chat with the boss once a year, and we have a chat with them. In some respects this is liked because there is nothing formal to fear. However, where we express a desire for, say, more training, we never know if it is going to happen; it is down to the interest shown by whoever is doing the interview. One member of staff said if you get an appraisal when the senior staff member is having a bad day you can end up going through a very negative experience.

Strengths – No fear attached normally; informal.

Weaknesses – No guarantee of action or continuity of process.

Opportunities – To use the system to get to know the desires of staff which may motivate them, and to discuss ways of doing jobs more efficiently.

Threats – The staff may get very demotivated if the appraisal seems a waste of time.

Action – Formalise the procedure.

Responsibility – Senior staff.

Priority – Low.

7   Solution – Development of business professionals

Findings – We have jobs not careers. Most staff are happy with this.

Strengths – It suits most people.

Weaknesses – It does not suit everyone.

Opportunities – Cannot see any at the moment.

Threats – We could lose staff if they see opportunities arising elsewhere.

Action – Cannot identify within the constraints of our firm.

Responsibility – N/A.

Priority – N/A.

Chapter 9

IMPROVING THE SYSTEM

1   Activity – Environmental considerations

Is there evidence that your firm understands the environment in which it operates?

Leads:

See if senior staff can identify the environment in which your firm operates.
Is this a stable or frequently changing environment?
Can they can explain the significance of the environment for the way your firm operates?
What is the significance for the way your accounting system operates?
Do you feel you and your firm are keeping up with the pace of environmental change?

Findings

Strengths

Weaknesses

Opportunities

Threats

Action

Responsibility

Priority

2   **Activity – Accounting information systems**

Has the structure of your firm affected the type of accountancy system in which you work ?

Leads:

Are any or all of your activities costed out per unit of activity?
Does your firm take such data and add it to that of other departments, so as to determine and compare the overall cost of that area of activity and that department?

Findings

Strengths

Weaknesses

Opportunities

Threats

Action

Responsibility

Priority

3   Activity – The evolution of management information systems

Can you see evidence that management information systems are currently evolving in your firm, or are they stagnant?

Leads:

Ask senior colleagues to identify management information systems.
Ask how they have changed and why over the last 5 years?
Is your system appropriate for your size of firm and the work you do?
Do you need a management information system within your accounting system?
Are decisions supported effectively by the information system?

Findings

Strengths

Weaknesses

Opportunities

Threats

Action

Responsibility

Priority

4   Activity – Control of management information systems

Is information technology contributing to corporate strategy?

Leads:

Is there a team which controls management information systems in your firm?
How are the team's members chosen?
How will fast-changing environments impact on the control process?
What kind of cost benefit assessments are required?
Do the benefits add up to something of real value for your firm?

Findings

Strengths

Weaknesses

Opportunities

Threats

Action

Responsibility

Priority

◆ FOULKS*lynch*

5   Activity – MIS and competitive advantage

How can an MIS help your firm to compete in the market place?

Leads:

To what extent do you need to compete? With whom and to what degree?
Are there threats of future competition? If yes, then where from and when?
How will the MIS be able to assist you in competing effectively?
Will an MIS help you to give a better service to your clients/customers?
Can you buy in the expertise?

Findings

Strengths

Weaknesses

Opportunities

Threats

Action

Responsibility

Priority

6   Activity – Influence on strategy

Is culture really a strategic consideration?

Leads:

How seriously does your firm take the subject of culture?
Is it ever discussed? Has culture a high enough profile?
Is there evidence it is brought into strategic planning?
Does your accounting systems culture fit easily into the firm's overall culture?
If not, why not, and what could be done to improve matters?
Do you think managers manage culture without realising it?
Is so, is there a way they could do it better?

Findings

Strengths

Weaknesses

Opportunities

Threats

Action

Responsibility

Priority

7   Activity – Culture and the individual

Does culture affect you, or do you affect culture?

Leads

Have you previously given much thought to culture?
Will you think about it from now on?
Do you need guidance? From whom?
How will you benefit from a personal study of your firm's culture?

Findings

Strengths

Weaknesses

Opportunities

Threats

Action

Responsibility

Priority

1 Solution – Environmental considerations

Findings – We never talk about the environment. There is one other agency in the town, and it is part of a major chain, but we don't talk about it as a threat to us. Most staff didn't understand what I meant about the environment, except Mr Turisst who showed little interest.

Strengths – None.

Weaknesses – Ignorance of the significance of the environment.

Opportunities – Unsure without further research.

Threats – From anyone who tries to put us out of business.

Action – Discuss the significance of our environment.

Responsibility – Senior staff.

Priority – High.

2 Solution – Accounting information systems

Findings – We do not have any effective accounting information systems. Mr Turisst is merely happy that he is earning a good profit, rather than seeking the best profit.

Strengths – We are making profit.

Weaknesses – We are missing out on possible expansion and business improvement.

Opportunities – To cost out the business and find out how to cut costs without cutting staff levels and quality of service. To improve staff prospects through expansion, and to make the business more profitable and so saleable at a higher price.

Threats – If another agency tried to compete on price, through special deals, we could be priced out of business. A new owner may reduce staff to cut costs.

Action – Establish an accounting system, which grows in sophistication in time.

Responsibility – Mr Turisst and senior staff, with consultation with all staff.

Priority – High.

3 Solution – The evolution of management information systems

As our severe lack of a management information system has already been established, I cannot really answer this.

4 Solution – Control of management information systems

No answer again.

Note to student – again do not worry about lack of findings. As before, the lack of information can be unsettling; in this section you find the missing list is growing..... but if that is how things are in your firm then you just have to flow with it. This is real life!

5   Solution – MIS and competitive advantage

Findings – Another job for the consultants! We have a definite void here.

6   Solution – Influence on strategy

I feel this will be a consideration for us if we are taken over by a chain, but not in our present state.

7   Solution – Culture and the individual.

Findings – Individual responses to the study of culture were vague and non-committal.

Strengths – There is group culture in existence.

Weaknesses – Individual culture is not seen as important.

Opportunities – To change our point of view as individuals.

Threats – Apathy.

Action – Think about our individual positions.

Responsibility – All staff.

Priority – Low.

Chapter 10–12

CONTROL SYSTEMS IN PRACTICE

INTERNAL CONTROL CHECKLISTS

Improving the effectiveness of an accounting system has many aspects, many of which have been covered in the chapters leading up to this one. Organisation, motivation etc are all important, and improvement in these areas can have lasting impacts on the way an accounting system or department works.

However, one of the core aspects of the efficiency and effectiveness of an accounting department is the internal controls that exist in such departments. In the absence of these fundamental controls, no amount of leadership or motivation can transform such a department into one that will ever perform satisfactorily.

In this section therefore we provide you with internal control checklists of all main areas in a typical accounting department.

You are not of course expected to examine and work your way through all these various elements. It will be preferable if you concentrate on one area, such as, sales and debtors or purchases and creditors, and work thoroughly through such an area. Talk to the relevant people in your own organisation and record your findings on the following checklists. This will provide the basis of a report covering the internal control aspects of a particular area under consideration. At the end of this section we are reproducing from the textbook the typical findings which such a review could result in.

INTERNAL CONTROL CHECKLIST – PURCHASES AND CREDITORS

(a)   **Orders**

    (i)   Requisition notes for purchases should be authorised.

    (ii)   All orders should be authorised by a responsible official whose authority limits should be pre-defined.

    (iii)   Major items e.g., capital expenditure, should be authorised by the board.

    (iv)   All orders should be recorded on official documents showing suppliers' names, quantities ordered and price.

    (v)   Copies of orders should be retained as a method of following up late deliveries by suppliers.

    (vi)   Re-order levels and quantities should be pre-set and preferably recorded in advance on the requisition note.

(b)   **Receipt of goods**

    (i)   Goods inwards centres should be identified to deal with the receipt of all goods.

    (ii)   All goods should be checked for quantity and quality. Goods received notes should be raised for all goods accepted. The GRN should be signed by a responsible official.

    (iii)   GRNs should be checked against purchase orders and procedures should exist to notify the supplier of under-or over-deliveries. GRNs should be sequentially numbered and checked periodically for completeness.

(c)   **Invoicing and returns**

    (i)   Purchase invoices received should be stamped with an approval grid and given a unique serial number to ensure purchase invoices do not go astray.

    (ii)   Purchase invoices should be matched with goods received notes and should not be processed until this is done.

    (iii)   The invoice should be checked against the order and the GRN, and casts and extensions should also be checked.

    (iv)   The invoices should be signed as approved for payment by a responsible official independent of the ordering and receipt of goods functions.

    (v)   Invoice sequential numbers should be checked against purchase day book details.

    (vi)   Input VAT should be separated from the expense.

    (vii)   Invoices should be properly allocated to the nominal ledger accounts, perhaps by allocating expenditure codes. A portion of such coding should be checked independently.

(viii)   Batch controls should be maintained over the posting of invoices to the purchases day book, nominal ledger and purchase ledger.

(ix)   A record of goods returned should be kept and checked to the credit notes received from suppliers.

(d)   **Purchase ledger and suppliers**

(i)   A purchase ledger control account should be maintained and regularly checked against balances in the ledger by an independent official.

(ii)   Purchase ledger records should be kept by persons independent of the receiving of goods, invoice authorisation and payment routines.

(iii)   Statements from suppliers should be checked against the purchase ledger account.

INTERNAL CONTROL CHECKLIST – SALES AND DEBTORS

There are a large number of controls that may be required in the sales cycle due to the importance of this area in any business and the possible opportunities that exist for diverting sales away from the business and other persons benefiting.

(a) **Orders**

    (i)   The orders should be checked against the customer's account; this should be evidenced by initialling. Any new customer should be referred to the credit control department before the order is accepted.

    (ii)   Existing customers should be allocated a credit limit and it should be ascertained whether this limit is to be exceeded if the new order is accepted. If so the matter should be referred to credit control.

    (iii)   All orders received should be recorded on pre-numbered sales order documents.

    (iv)   All orders should be authorised before any goods are despatched.

    (v)   The sales order should be used to produce a despatch note for the goods outwards department. No goods may be despatched without a despatch note.

(b) **Despatch**

    (i)   Despatch notes should be pre-numbered and a register kept of them to relate to sales invoices and orders.

    (ii)   Goods despatch notes should be authorised as goods leave and checked periodically to ensure they are complete and that all have been invoiced.

(c) **Invoicing and credit notes**

    (i)   Sales invoices should be authorised by a responsible official and referenced to the original authorised order and despatch note.

    (ii)   All invoices and credit notes should be entered in sales day book records, the sales ledger, and sales ledger control account. Batch totals should be maintained for this purpose.

    (iii)   Sales invoices and credit notes should be checked for prices, casts and calculations by a person other than the one preparing the invoice.

    (iv)   All invoices and credit notes should be serially pre-numbered and regular sequence checks should be carried out.

    (v)   Credit notes should be authorised by someone unconnected with despatch or sales ledger functions.

    (vi)   Copies of cancelled invoices should be retained.

    (vii)   Any invoice cancellation should lead to a cancellation of the appropriate despatch note.

Comments

(viii) Cancelled and free of charge invoices should be signed by a responsible official.

(ix) Each invoice should distinguish between different types of sales and VAT. Any coding of invoices should be periodically checked independently.

(d) **Returns**

(i) Any goods returned by the customer should be checked for obvious damage and, when accepted, a document should be raised.

(ii) All goods returned should be used to prepare appropriate credit notes.

(e) **Debtors**

(i) A sales ledger control account should be prepared regularly and checked to individual sales ledger balances by an independent official.

(ii) Sales ledger personnel should be independent of despatch and cash receipt functions.

(iii) Statements should be sent regularly to customers.

(iv) Formal procedures should exist for following up overdue debts which should be highlighted either by the preparation of an aged list of balances or in the preparation of statements to customers.

(v) Letters should be sent to customers for collection of overdue debts.

(f) **Bad debts**

(i) The authority to write off a bad debt should be given in writing and adjustments made to the sales ledger.

(ii) The use of court action or the writing-off of a bad debt should be authorised by an official independent of the cash receipt function.

INTERNAL CONTROL CHECKLIST – WAGES AND SALARIES

(a)   **Approval and control of documents**

    (i)   There should be written authorisation to employ or dismiss any employee.

    (ii)   Changes in rates of pay should be authorised in writing by an official outside the wages department.

    (iii)   Overtime worked should be authorised by the works manager/supervisor.

    (iv)   An independent official should check the payroll and sign it.

    (v)   The wages cheque should be signed by two signatories evidenced against the signed payroll.

    (vi)   Where weekly pay relates to hours at work, clock cards should be used. There should be supervision of the cards and the timing devices, particularly when employees are clocking-on or off.

    (vii)   Personnel records should be kept for each employee giving details of engagement, retirement, dismissal or resignation, rates of pay, holidays etc, with a specimen signature of the employee.

    (viii)   A wages supervisor should be appointed who could perform some of the authorisation duties listed above.

(b)   **Arithmetical accuracy**

    (i)   Payroll should be prepared from clock cards, job cards etc, and a sample checked for accuracy against current rates of pay.

    (ii)   Payroll details should provide for the accurate calculation of deductions e.g., PAYE, NI, pensions, trade union subscriptions etc, which should be checked periodically.

(c)   **Control accounts**

    (i)   Control accounts should be maintained in respect of each of the deductions showing amounts paid periodically to the Revenue, trade unions etc.

    (ii)   Overall checks should be carried out to highlight major discrepancies e.g., check against budgets, changes in amounts paid over a period of time, check against personnel records.

    (iii)   Management should exercise overall control.

(d)   **Access to assets and records**

    (i)   An employee should sign for his wages.

    (ii)   No employee should be allowed to take the wages of another employee.

Comments

(iii)   When wages are claimed late, the employee should sign for the wage packet and the release of the packet should be authorised.

(iv)   The system should preferably allow the wages to be checked by the employee before the packet is opened, by using specially designed wage packets.

(v)   The wages department should preferably be a separate department with their personnel not involved with receipts or payments functions.

(vi)   The duties of the wages staff should preferably be rotated during the year, and ensure that no employee is responsible for all the functions in respect of any particular department.

(vii)   The employee making up the pay packets should not be the employee who prepares the payroll.

(viii)   A surprise attendance at the pay-out should be made periodically by an independent official.

(ix)   Unclaimed wages should be recorded in a register and held by someone outside the wages department until claimed or until a predefined period after which the money should be rebanked. An official should investigate the reason for unclaimed wages as soon as possible.

(e)   **Salaries**

(i)   Personnel records should be kept similar to those for hourly paid employees.

(ii)   Written authority should be required to employ or dismiss an employee or change salary rate.

(iii)   Overtime should be authorised by someone outside the payroll department.

(iv)   The usual checks on deductions are required.

(v)   When an employee has been absent for a significant period his entitlement to salary should be checked against personnel details.

(vi)   Cheques should have two signatories and should be checked against an approved payroll entry.

(vii)   Direct bank transfers should also be signed and checked regularly against details on personnel files.

INTERNAL CONTROL CHECKLIST – CASH AND BANKINGS

(a)   **Controls over cash receipts by post**

(i)   The company should safeguard against possible interceptions between the receipt and opening of the post e.g., by using a locked mail box and restricting access to the keys.

(ii)   The opening of the post should be supervised by a responsible official and where the volume of mail is significant, at least two persons should be present when the mail is opened.

(iii)   All cheques and postal orders should be restrictively crossed 'Account payee only, not negotiable' as soon as the mail is opened.

(iv)   A record should be made at the time of the opening of the post of:

–   cheques and postal orders received
–   cash received.

This record may be in the form of a rough cash book, adding machine list or copies of remittance advices.   It provides control over the eventual sums banked and entered into the cash book.

(v)   The cashier and sales ledger personnel should not have access to the receipts before this record is made.

(vi)   Post should be date stamped.   It provides evidence of when remittances are received and can periodically be checked against the date of banking.   This helps to prevent cash received one day being banked as representing different receipts on a later day (a process known as 'teeming and lading').

(b)   **Controls over cash collected by salesmen and travellers**

(i)   Authority to collect cash should be clearly defined.

(ii)   Salesmen and travellers should be required to remit cash and report sales at regular intervals which should be formally notified to such employees.

(iii)   A responsible official should quickly follow up salesmen who do not submit returns as required.

(iv)   Collections should be recorded when received e.g., in a rough cash book or copies of receipts which should be given to the salesmen or travellers.

(v)   The collector's cash receipts should be reconciled to the eventual banking.

(vi)   Periodically a responsible official should check the salesmen's own receipt books with cash book entries.

(vii)   If salesmen hold stocks of goods, an independent reconciliation of stock with sales and cash received should be made.

(c)   **Controls over cash sales**

(i)   Cash sales should be recorded when the sale is made normally by means of a cash till or the use of cash sale invoices.

(ii)   If cash sale invoices are used they should be pre-numbered, a register should be maintained of cash sale invoice books and copies should be retained.

(iii)   Cash received should be reconciled daily with either the till roll or the invoice totals.

(iv)   This reconciliation should be carried out by someone independent of those receiving the cash and recording the sale.

(v)   Daily banking should be checked against the till roll or invoice total and differences investigated.

(vi)   A responsible official should sign cancelled cash sale invoices at the time of cancellation. All such invoices should be checked periodically for sequential numbering.

(d)   **Controls over banking**

(i)   Receipts should be banked intact daily.

(ii)   Each day's receipts should be recorded promptly in the cash book.

(iii)   Sales ledger personnel should have no access to the cash or the preparation of the paying-in slip.

(iv)   Periodically a comparison should be made between the split of cash and cheques:

–   received (and recorded in rough cash book)
–   banked (and recorded on paying-in slip).

(e)   **Controls over cheque payments**

(i)   Unused cheques should be held in a secure place.

(ii)   The person who prepares cheques should have no responsibility over purchase ledger or sales ledger.

(iii)   Cheques should be signed only when evidence of a properly approved transaction is available. Such evidence may take the form of invoices, payroll, petty cash book etc.

(iv)   This check should be evidenced by signing the supporting documentation.

(v)   In a large concern those approving the original document should be independent of those signing cheques.

(vi)   Cheque signatories should be restricted to the minimum practical number.

(vii)   Two signatories at least should be required except perhaps for cheques of small amounts.

(viii) The signing of blank cheques and cheques in favour of the signatory should be prohibited.

(ix)   Cheques should be crossed before being signed.

(x)   Supporting documents should be cancelled as paid to prevent their use to support further cheque payments. This cancellation could be done by the cashier before the cheque is signed (provided the cancellation identifies the cheque number) or by the cheque signatory at the time of signing the cheque.

(xi)   Cheques should preferably be despatched immediately. If not, they should be held in a safe place.

(xii) Returned cheques may be obtained from the bank and a sample checked against cash book entries and supporting documentation.

(f) Bank reconciliations

(i)   Bank reconciliations should be prepared at least monthly.

(ii)   The person responsible for preparation should be independent of the receipts and payments function or, alternatively, an independent person should check the reconciliation.

(iii) If the reconciliation is prepared by an independent person he should obtain bank statements directly from the bank and hold them until the reconciliation is completed.

(iv)   The preparation should preferably include a check of at least a sample of receipts and payments against items on the bank statement.

(g) Controls over petty cash

(i)   The level and location of cash floats should be laid down formally.

(ii)   There should be restricted access to the floats.

(iii) Cash should be securely held e.g., in a locked drawer, with restricted access to keys.

(iv)   All expenditure should require a voucher signed by a responsible official, not the petty cashier.

(v)   The imprest system should be used to reimburse the float ie, at any time the total cash and value of vouchers not reimbursed equals a set amount.

(vi)   Vouchers should be produced before the cheque is signed for reimbursement.

(vii) Vouchers should be cancelled once reimbursement has taken place.

(viii) A maximum amount should be placed on a petty cash payment to discourage normal purchase procedures being by-passed.

(ix)   Periodically the petty cash should be reconciled by an independent person.

(x)   Rules should exist preferably preventing the issue of IOU's or
        the cashing of cheques.

INTERNAL CONTROL CHECKLIST – STOCK

(a)   **Approval and control of documents**

    (i)   Issues from stocks should be made only on properly authorised requisitions.

    (ii)   Reviews of damaged, obsolete and slow moving stock should be carried out. Any write-offs should be authorised.

(b)   **Arithmetical accuracy**

    (i)   All receipts and issues should be recorded on stock cards, cross-referenced to the appropriate GRN or requisition document.

    (ii)   The costing department should allocate direct and overhead costs to the value of work-in-progress according to the stage of completion reached.

    (iii)   To do this standard costs are normally used. Such standards must be regularly reviewed to ensure that they relate to actual costs being incurred.

    (iv)   If the value of work-in-progress is directly comparable with the number of units produced, checks should periodically be made of actual units against work-in-progress records.

(c)   **Control accounts**

    (i)   Total stock records may be maintained and integrated with the main accounting system; if so they should be reconciled to detailed stock records and discrepancies investigated.

(d)   **Comparison of assets to records**

    (i)   Stock levels should be periodically checked against the records by a person independent of the stores personnel, and material differences investigated.

    (ii)   Where continuous stock records are not kept adequately a full stocktake should be held at least once a year.

    (iii)   Maximum and minimum stock levels should be pre-determined and regularly reviewed for adequacy.

    (iv)   Re-order quantities should be pre-determined and regularly reviewed for adequacy.

(e)   **Access to assets and records**

    (i)   Separate centres should be identified at which goods are held.

    (ii)   Deliveries of goods from suppliers should pass through a goods inwards section to the stores. All goods should pass through stores and hence be recorded and checked as received.

    (iii)   Stocks should be held in their locations so that they are safe from damage or theft.

(iv)   All stock lines should be identified and held together e.g., in bins which are marked with all relevant information as to size, grade, origin, title for identification.

(v)   Access to the stores should be restricted.

INTERNAL CONTROL CHECKLIST – FIXED ASSETS

(a)   Annual capital expenditure budgets should be prepared by someone directly responsible to the board of directors.

(b)   Such budgets should, if acceptable, be agreed by the board and minuted.

(c)   Applications for authority to incur capital expenditure should be submitted to the board for approval and should contain reasons for the expenditure, estimated cost, and any fixed assets replaced.

(d)   A document should show what is to be acquired and be signed as authorised by the board or an authorised official.

(e)   Capital projects made by the company itself should be separately identifiable in the company's costing records and should reflect direct costs plus relevant overhead but not include any profit.

(f)   Disposal of fixed assets should be authorised and any proceeds from sale should be related to the authority.

(g)   A register of fixed assets should be maintained for each major group of assets. The register should identify each item within that group and contain details of cost and depreciation.

(h)   A physical inspection of fixed assets should be carried out periodically and checked to the fixed asset register. Any discrepancies should be noted and investigated.

(i)   Assets should be properly maintained and adequately insured.

(j)   Depreciation rates should be authorised and a written statement of policy produced.

(k)   Depreciation should be reviewed annually to assess the need for changes in the light of profits or losses on disposal, new technology etc.

(l)   The calculation of depreciation should be checked for accuracy.

(m)   Fixed assets should be reviewed for the need for any write-down.

TYPICAL REPORT ON FINDINGS FOLLOWING REVIEW OF AN ACCOUNTING SYSTEM

◈ FOULKS*lynch*

REVIEW OF CONTROLS IN SYSTEMS

UPPER PLC – YEAR ENDED 31 DECEMBER 200X

(a)   **Payroll**

Weakness:

No evidence of approval.

Implications:

Unauthorised changes may occur.

Recommendations:

Management should evidence their approval of the payroll, changes in rates of pay and the employment of new staff.

(b)   **Stock**

Weakness:

Lack of physical and financial control over stocks.
Cut-off errors were discovered for widgets despatched prior to the year end but uninvoiced.
Overhead allocation in valuation of widgets lacked support.

Implications:

Stock could be misappropriated.
The year end stock figure could be misstated.

Recommendations:

(i)   A simple system of perpetual inventory should be implemented at each location. This should be used to check for the despatch and receipt of stock and would provide good overall control to enable a comparison of:

–   expected use to actual by comparison with orders; and

–   book stock to actual after regular stock checks.

(ii)   Improvements should be made to the system of control to facilitate a review of the despatches at the year end to ensure that a proper cut-off is achieved.

(iii)   The valuation of widgets depends on the estimated throughput during the year. It is important that the number of widgets produced is properly recorded and that consideration is given to normal production levels to allow compliance with SSAP 9.

(c)   **Fixed assets**

Weakness:

Lack of physical control.
Lack of clear capitalisation policy.

Assets with nil net book value were subject to a depreciation charge.

Implications:

Portable assets could be misappropriated.
Items could be incorrectly capitalised.
The depreciation figures in the accounts could be overstated.

Recommendations:

(i)   A register should be introduced to record all assets at cost together with associated depreciation.

(ii)   In previous years capital additions, notably the improvements to the leasehold premises, have been written off. Also, assets scrapped have not been written off. The effect of these cancel out and therefore we have not proposed an adjustment to opening figures. A capitalisation policy should be laid down and adhered to.

(iii)   A register would enable the identification of fully depreciated assets and allow them to be excluded from the depreciation calculations.

(d)   **Purchases payments**

Weakness:

Lack of proper allocation of costs.
Lack of supporting documents.
Lack of control over cheque books.
Unauthorised charges.
Poor control over unrecorded liabilities.

Implications:

Purchases in the accounts may be misstated.
Creditors may be understated if unrecorded liabilities are not controlled.

Recommendations:

(i)   All charges incurred should be allocated to the relevant cost centre to promote accountability of these centres.

(ii)   Proper supporting documents for all payments must be retained and properly filed for easy retrieval.

(iii)   Control over payments would be improved if only one cheque book was in use at any one time.

(iv)   Documents supporting charges should be authorised by an appropriate level of management.

(v)   A purchase day book should be introduced. Payments should be marked off. This would provide control over unpaid invoices and a means for regular control account reconciliation.

Prepared by:

Date:

Chapter 13

FRAUD MANAGEMENT

1 Activity – Introduction

Is fraud a matter for me to be concerned with?

Leads:

Who needs to know about fraud policies?
What exactly is fraud anyway?
What are the fraud policies in your firm?

Findings

Strengths

Weaknesses

Opportunities

Threats

Action

Responsibility

Priority

2 Activity – How does fraud occur?

Can we identify the areas of risk in our firm?

Leads:

Who might commit a fraud?
How could they do it?
Why would they do it?

Findings

Strengths

Weaknesses

Opportunities

Threats

Action

Responsibility

Priority

3   Activity – Managing risk

Do we need to learn new management skills?

Leads:

Who should be responsible for risk management?
Who actually is in your firm?
What controls exist?
Does anyone evaluate the success of controls?

Findings

Strengths

Weaknesses

Opportunities

Threats

Action

Responsibility

Priority

4   Activity – Methods of fraud prevention and detection

Is prevention better than cure?

Leads:

What steps are taken in your firm to prevent fraud?
Are procedures adhered to?
Do staff believe fraud controls are effective?
Are you personally vigilant against the risk of fraud?

Findings

Strengths

Weaknesses

Opportunities

Threats

Action

Responsibility

Priority

5   Activity – Fraud response plans

How do you respond to fraud, potential and actual?

Leads:

Do fraud response plans exist?
Do they need to be written or re-written?
Who needs to know their contents? Why?

Findings

Strengths

Weaknesses

Opportunities

Threats

Action

Responsibility

Priority

1   Solution – Introduction

Findings – The term fraud was not readily understood in the context of our work, but without knowing it they were concerned about fraud. For example, foreign exchange clerks locked their tills in their absence, and the accounts team carried out standard security routines. No known cases of fraud to date.

Strengths – Appreciation of the risk, and contra activity.

Weaknesses – Limited knowledge.

Opportunities – To learn more.

Threats – Apathy; misunderstanding.

Action – Fraud awareness course.

Responsibility – Senior staff to arrange; me to deliver as I am studying this

Priority – Medium.

2   Solution – How does fraud occur?

Findings – Limited knowledge of how fraud occurs.

Strengths – Few (some knowledge).

Weaknesses – Limited knowledge = limited protection.

Opportunities – To learn.

Threats – From anyone who thinks we are slack enough to be breached.

Action – Fraud awareness course.

Responsibility – Senior staff to arrange; me to deliver as I am studying this.

Priority – Medium.

3   Solution – Managing risk

Findings – We do not manage it; it is left to individuals to be vigilant.

Strengths – Some management of risk.

Weaknesses – Largely unplanned and uncoordinated.

Opportunities – To set up formal risk management policies and procedures.

Threats – Apathy.

Action – Policy statements and procedures.

Responsibility – Senior staff.

Priority – Medium.

4   Solution – Methods of fraud prevention and detection

Findings – We have not got as far as this yet in our learning curve or procedures - needs to be re-examined after we have had more training.

5   Solution – Fraud response plans

Findings – None exist – another area to re-visit.

CASE STUDY

FINAL REPORT

To: Connor Turisst
From: James Berry – Accounts Section leader

Subject: Increasing efficiency at Sealandair

Terms of reference: To find ways of improving efficiency in the firm, without the need for dedicating a large volume of resources pre-sale.

Methods

Interviews – face to face:

–   individual basis
–   section groups
–   cross section groups
–   individual questionnaires
–   section questionnaires.

Time span: 3 months

1   FINDINGS

1.1   Introduction

Sealandair is a firm which has remained essentially unchanged for many years, and will need to take many actions, some of them drastic, in order to obtain optimum efficiency levels of operation. As the firm is due to be sold in the near future, it is unlikely that all of the changes required can be enacted before the sale takes place, and it is probable that the resources required to effect this change could not be recouped on sale.

1.2   Structural dimensions of the organisation

Sealandair operates without reference to environmental factors. There is little competition in the town where the business is based, and staff do not understand the significance of environmental impact, and the owner has little interest.

As the firm is not part of a chain, there is not a significant centralisation-decentralisation question to address. Staff are allowed to operate freely, but have expressed a desire for more co-ordination.

In this small firm working relationships are well understood without the need to chart them, and staff are fully aware of formal reporting lines.

The firm is run on informal lines, so this informality is unplanned and arises from managerial apathy. Colleagues are able to work together. However they would welcome a higher degree of formality which would facilitate co-operation between themselves on a known and reliable basis.

A basic functional structure exists, and works quite well, but its future suitability will be a function of the environment continuing to remain stable. It is thought that any future change to structure would be problematic for the staff, as they have worked for many years within the existing structure.

1.3   Organisational structure, performance and change

The nature and function of the organisation cannot be attributed to the theory of any particular management science professional. The business is very individual. It is understood that should the business be sold to an existing chain of agencies, it would have to adopt that new and overriding nature and function.

The firm does not operate on a systems management basis, and staff have not devoted time to this area of management. Staff are organised into specialist sections, facilitating expertise in their operations, however the facility does not assist to cross cover roles, which sometimes results in they need to employ expensive external temporary staff.

There is evidence that staff do not subordinate their own interests to that of the firm, and that this has an adverse effect on efficiency levels.

There is no evidence of the existence of an effective accounting information system, the owner is content that a good profit is being made, rather than seeking to maximise profit.

Staff understand the meaning of efficiency and effectiveness, but readily admit that they cannot measure the degrees that have been achieved. Furthermore, there is very little understanding of the difference between development of the business and its growth.

This is not a learning organisation, the staff appreciating the need to learn about the procedures involved in their own work, but essentially carrying on their business in the same way as they always have done.

1.4   Information technology and organisational structure

The computer systems are dated, but serve procedural needs. There is doubt over the system's ability to handle an accounting information system.

Because of the inadequacy of Information Systems, the relationship between benefits and costs cannot be determined, as the firm's cost structure cannot be determined.

It is not felt that too much information is generated internally, and where the lack of management information is highlighted, the problem exists that the staff are not sure what management information they should have.

All staff feel that constant advice is required regarding their data processing system needs.

1.5   Strategic elements

Apart from the owner wanting to generate profit, there is no developing strategy, and there are very few skills in respect of implementing strategy.

There is some evidence of contingency planning, but normally problems are dealt with as they arise, rather than planning being utilised to avoid them.

Staff are good at making decisions when problems arise, especially considering the primitive nature of their systems, but still too many problems arise due to lack of planning.

Budgeting is used as a control method, operating via a standard costing system with variance analysis. However, there is a total ignorance of budgeting in respect of quality related costs.

1.6   Management control systems

There is no major formal strategy for organisational control, rather staff obey the instructions as given out by senior staff. Senior staff appreciate that they would not know how to build a management information system, and would need external help. Any system obtained would need to operate on a small scale, and staff training would be required.

1.7   Management: nature, style and motivation

Senior staff believe they are effective as managers to a certain degree, because they have been running the business for many years. They do appreciate that improvements could be made.

Many different styles of management are in evidence as a function of task importance, staff member executing the task, and prevailing circumstances. Some styles are more effective than others, and those managing have a different perception of their style effectiveness to those who are being managed.

The staff are motivated in numerous ways, and one motivation element has not been identified. Increased pay has been identified, but not as a serious motivation element. Staff indicated that a potential core elements exists in terms of job security, fair treatment from senior staff and good working atmosphere. The owner is motivated by a future sale of the business, at a good price, followed by retirement on the Continent.

The firm has managed to escape the harsh conditions that exist in other organisations, and staff do not wish to undergo radical change unless they can be part of the decision making process.

Formal quality systems do not exist, though staff do their best for customers, and customers do return year after year.

1.8   Personnel planning

There is no personnel department in this small firm, but staff feel they are treated in a humane way; not as a resource. There is evidence of lack of manpower planning in that cover is sometimes difficult when staff are absent.

Individual objectives are not set, except the owner requires staff to work hard and make the business money, which they strive to do.

Staff are not sure if they need to be developed, only showing vague interest in new computerised systems. Appraisals are poorly handled, in that the decisions for action that arise are not always followed through.

The staff do not perceive themselves as having careers; they are happy to have jobs.

1.9   Leadership and decision making

There is an absence of leadership, in the sense of there being no direction given towards new areas of activity or improved working practices.

There is no training given on decision making and problem solving techniques, no formal method of prioritising activity, and no assessment of the quality and speed of decisions made.

When decisions are made, staff feel that they know how far they can go without seeking higher authority.

1.10   Group dynamics

There are formal planned groups, for example the accounts team. Social groupings, for example at lunch time, can be cross functional. The cross functional groups give rise to gossip and rumour, and staff act differently in informal groups to when they are in their formal functional groups.

Staff express a need to belong to a group, stating that the social aspect is motivating, as is the membership of a different group to their normal functional group.

Staff feel that they are effective within their own jobs, but appreciate that they could be missing out on better practices.

1.11   Communication: role, style and barriers

Staff admit that they are not as good at listening as they are at talking. There are very few matters of communication, and those used are unstructured. The need for screen placed communication has been mentioned.

Communication is not seen as a process, and so is not planned. Feedback is not regularly given to confirm understanding, which leads to problems arising.

Briefing sessions are utilised, but staff were unaware of the use of quality circles.

1.12   Authority and conflict

Senior staff feel they have power over junior staff. They see their acts of delegation as being to free time for higher duties, but junior staff see delegation as work dumping.

Staff feel they know their place in the firm, and normally accept requests from each other. There are some rows, but are seen as positive as they clear the air, and it is felt that the staff know each other too well to seriously disagree on a long term basis or in a way averse to teamwork.

There is conflict between work groups, as a result of different priorities.

1.13   Time management

There is much time wasted in the firm, without any realisation of the cost which attaches. There is little planning of time, and frequently problems meeting schedules.

Staff, including senior staff, were very surprised to see how many leaks there were once they knew what to look for. Hardly any time management techniques were known.

1.14   Fraud management

The term fraud was not understood in the context of the work carried out, according to the responses of staff, though in practice they did show a level of concern, for example as seen when foreign exchange clerks locked their tills in times of absence from their counters.

Staff have limited knowledge of how fraud occurs, and risk is not managed, but rather left to the vigilance of individuals. An operational risk management checklist was shown to staff, and the general consensus was that the firm failed the checklist significantly. Fraud response plans are non-existent.

Specific problems with purchase system

The computerised accounts system automatically opens up a creditor account without any responsible official authorising it. This could lead to fictitious accounts being created or fraudulent purchase transactions.

Purchase invoices are not authorised before being posted to the purchase ledger. This could lead to liabilities being created for incorrect or fictitious purchases.

Cheques are created and sent out without authority. These cheques could be for incorrect amounts or made payable to the wrong supplier or be payable to fictitious suppliers.

2   RECOMMENDATIONS FOR ACTION

2.1   Introduction

Sealandair is not operating as an efficient business should. It has survived up until the present day, but this is due to its position in a stable environment, and the loyalty of staff, rather than due to sound operational management.

2.2   Environment and structure

The senior staff, and especially the owner, should have taken greater account of the environment in which they operate, so as to ensure the business keeps up with the changing demands of time, and that it can cope with any competition it might face.

The lack of planned formality has some advantages, but leads to a position where dynamism is suppressed. The overall structure of the firm needs defining and formalising.

2.3   Systems

Sealandair should improve its information systems and assess its own efficiency and effectiveness. Opportunities for development and growth are being missed, as is the chance for the firm to evolve into a more efficient unit.

Computerised systems should be upgraded to assist in both communication and information provision. The firm must use such systems to assess its own cost structure, so that it can further assess the value of benefits arising from changes in its activity.

2.4   Strategy and planning

Serious attention must be given to the business of planning, especially contingency planning, and staff must be taught how to make decisions and solve problems effectively and at speed.

The current standard budget control system is inadequate, and its upgrading again depends upon upgrading of Information Systems and computer systems.

There are insufficient skills within the firm to cope with the design of systems, and external consultants will need to be brought in to the firm.

Regarding the nature of management, all aspects of management within the firm are very weak. Apart from the planning deficiencies already mentioned, managers are ineffective due to a lack of application of management techniques.

2.5 Management

Styles of management vary from senior staff member to senior staff member, with varying degrees of efficiency. Attempts should be made to standardise management styles.

The significance of quality management, in respect of the external customer and the internal customer needs to be understood and staff trained in its practices.

2.6 Personnel issues

A process of effective human resource management does not exist and should be implemented. The human resource is very poorly applied to the firm's activities, and there are no firm objectives for individual staff members to pursue. These issues should be addressed.

An effective appraisal system should be introduced to direct staff toward performance improvement, or to facilitate the support of good practice from the individual.

There is in existence a system of delegation according to the perception of management, though it is obviously not a true delegation system. There should be a far more planned approach, and training to ensure that delegees are sufficiently trained to handle work passed to them.
Organisational conflicts exists, some of which is positive for the firm. However there are destructive conflicts which management should act to prevent.

2.7 Time management

Time is not managed effectively in this firm, probably because there is a lack of understanding of the cost to the firm of such waste. Even if this was understood, staff do not appreciate ways in which time is wasted, nor do they know how to correct the position. This should be addressed.

2.8 Fraud management

The firms attitude towards fraud and risk management is very poor, and a fraudster should find it reasonably easy to target this firm. This needs to be addressed, in particular with reference to the purchase system.

Particular problem with purchases system

New creditor accounts should only be opened after on-line authorisation by a senior employee.

All purchase invoices should be authorised prior to posting to the purchase ledger.

All cheques should be raised and authorised by different individuals. The authoriser should check supporting documentation prior to signing.

3 CONCLUSIONS

This is a firm in major difficulties, requiring an allocation of significant amounts of financial and human resource toward the achievement of modernisation.

The present owner does not have sufficient interest in the firm to achieve this, the senior staff do not have the skills to make it happen, the staff in general probably could not cope with such major changes. The imminent sale of the business would probably discourage the present owner from entering into such a major organisational project.

There are only two recommendations which can be made given the findings and conclusions drawn:

(1)   Sell the business as soon as possible, before a commercial disaster can reduce its sale value.

        The sale will almost certainly result in the changes required being implemented rapidly. A large chain could provide replacement human resources, and would have sufficient financial resources to make the improvements demanded.

(2)   Retain ownership of the business on a long-term basis, and implement long-term strategies to address the firm's many failings.

This approach may save the business in the long-term, but would not make commercial sense in terms of the financial reward being almost certainly less than the cost of improvement.

ADDITIONAL SCENARIOS AND REPORTS

ADDITIONAL SCENARIOS AND REPORTS

1   Activity

Burnden Ltd manufactures a range of components and spare parts for the textile industry. The company employs 150 hourly-paid production workers and 20 administrative staff, including the three directors of the company. There are two wages clerks who deal with the weekly payroll of the hourly-paid employees. They are directly responsible to the assistant accountant.

The company uses a computerised time clock at the factory gate to record the hours worked by the production employees. Each employee has a card with a magnetic strip with his own identification code on it. This card is inserted in the computerised time clock on the arrival and departure of the workers, whereupon it records the hours worked on the card. The cards are collected weekly by the wages clerks, who simply insert them individually into the microcomputer, which then reads them and prepares the payroll. The production manager keeps the unused clock cards in a locked cabinet in his office.

Wages are paid one week in arrears. The wages clerks compile the payroll by means of the microcomputer system, pass the payroll to the assistant accountant who scrutinises it before drawing the wages cheque, which is passed to one of the directors for signature. Any pay increases are negotiated locally by representatives of the employees. If any alterations are required to the standing data on the microcomputer, then the wages clerks amend the records. For example, when a wage increase has been negotiated, the rates of pay are changed by the wages clerks.

The cheque is drawn to cover net wages and the cashier makes arrangements for collecting the cash from the bank. The wages clerks then make up the wages envelopes. Whenever there is assistance required on preparing wages, the assistant accountant helps the wages clerks. The payment of wages is carried out by the production manager who returns any unclaimed wages to the wages clerks who keep them in a locked filing cabinet. Each employee is expected to collect his unclaimed wages personally.

New production employees are notified to the wages department verbally by the production manager and when employees leave, a note to that effect is sent to the wages department by the production manager. All statutory deductions are paid to the appropriate authorities by the chief accountant.

Administrative staff are paid monthly by credit transfer to their bank account. The payroll is prepared by the assistant accountant and the bank credit transfers are authorised by a director. Any increases in the salaries of the administrative staff are notified to the assistant accountant verbally by the chief accountant. The employment of administrative staff is authorised by the financial director.

You have recently been appointed the auditor of Burnden Ltd for the year ended 31 December 200X and have just started your interim audit. You are about to commence your audit evaluation and testing of the wages system.

Task

Prepare a schedule which details the weaknesses in the present wages and salaries system, the possible effect of such weaknesses, and suggest, with reasons, improvements which could be made to the system (assuming that the only controls are those set out above).

2   Activity

Appendex Ltd merchandises ladies footwear. The company purchases the bulk of its goods from British suppliers and uses a minicomputer system to record its business transactions. The computer department is located in the same office as the purchasing department and comprises the following personnel:

(i)   Mr Southfork, a systems analyst and programmer who is in charge of the department.

(ii)   Mrs Greenwood, a skilled programmer who also acts as a machine operator when the department is busy.

(iii)   Miss Wood, an assistant programmer and operator.

The computer software was purchased from a software house and was modified solely by Mr Southfork who kept the results of the testing of the modified programs for security reasons.

The purchasing department is managed by Mr Barnes, who is solely responsible for the placing of footwear orders. Purchase orders are provisionally fixed by telephone with suppliers and confirmed by Mr Barnes by telex. Mr Barnes lists the orders placed on a weekly basis and this list is used to update the stock file. The lead time between ordering and receipt of goods is normally fourteen days.

On receipt of the goods, the warehouseman makes out a prenumbered four-part goods received note set. One copy is given to the carrier as evidence of delivery of the goods, one copy each is sent to the purchasing department and the accounts department, whilst the final copy remains in the warehouse. Goods received notes are sent directly to Mr Barnes in the purchasing department.

When the accounts department receives the invoice, it is sent to Mr Barnes to authorise it and he checks the details to a copy of the telex order, and the goods received note. Further, after he has checked the details, he gives the documents to a member of his staff who checks the arithmetical accuracy of the invoice. If there is any discrepancy between it and the order and the goods received note, Mr Barnes alters the invoice by hand, and sends the invoice back to the accounts department who enter the amended amount on the purchase ledger input document which is sent to Mr Southfork.

On a weekly basis, Mrs Greenwood or Miss Wood loads the purchase ledger file which is held on magnetic disk and updates it from the input documentation received from the accounts department. The purchase ledger and an age listing of creditors is printed out once a month, and the stock ledger twice a month. These printouts are sent in the first instance to Mr Barnes who reviews them. Any exceptions which are apparent either in the review of the purchase ledger and stock file or because of processing problems are re-input only after Mr Barnes has given his authority. If input is rejected because there is no purchase ledger account on the disk, then Mr Southfork sets up an account and re-inputs the data himself.

Mr Southfork feels that he is very security conscious and dumps the files on the magnetic disk on to another disk on a weekly basis. This disk is kept in his desk drawer, and after one week the disk is overwritten. Mr Barnes determines which creditors are to be paid by making a manual listing of payments which is sent to the cashier. The cashier compares this listing to a copy of the purchase ledger print-out in order to verify the authenticity of the amount, and manually makes out the cheques which are signed by two directors. The directors scrutinise the listing of creditors for payment, before signing the cheques, and refuse to authorise any payment unless this listing has been signed by Mr Barnes and the cashier. Once the cheques have been signed, the payments listing is coded on to input documentation and sent to the computer department for processing. Any rejections of payment data are referred back to Mr Barnes who reviews the reason for the rejection, corrects it and re-inputs the data.

If goods are returned to the suppliers, a goods returns note is made out by the warehouseman in duplicate. One copy is returned with the goods, and the other copy is retained in the warehouse. When a credit note is received directly by Mr Barnes, he authorises it and the accounts department includes the value on the purchase invoice input sheet, and indicates the fact that it is a credit note by entering the amount in red ink on the list.

Task

Prepare a weakness schedule detailing the weaknesses in the purchases and creditors system and make recommendations for their improvement (assume that the only controls are those stated above).

1   Solution

| **Client:** | **Burnden Ltd** | **W/P Ref:** | **F1/2** |
| **Y/E Date:** | **31/12/0X** | | |

Prepared by: RRT
Date: 1/5/0X
Reviewed by: GL
Date: 5/5/0X

WEAKNESS	EFFECT	RECOMMENDATIONS
The wages clerks appear to amend pay rates without any authorisation.	Unauthorised changes could occur resulting in incorrect salary payments.	Changes in rates of pay should be authorised in writing by an official outside the wages department.
There are two wages clerks dealing with the production payroll.	There is too much reliance on individual employees; at present if one is absent those duties cannot be performed by the other.	To improve control within the wages department, the duties of these clerks should be rotated during the year. Neither of the clerks should be responsible for all the functions in the department.
Personnel records are not currently maintained for individual employees.	These records are essential and at present could not be recreated in the event of failure/corruption of the computer system.	Personnel records should be kept for each employee giving details of engagement, retirement, dismissal or resignation, rates of pay, holidays etc. with a specimen signature for the employee.
The production manager verbally notifies the wages department of new employees.	As the production manager also controls the unused clock cards and pays out the wages, fictitious employees could be introduced undetected.	There should be written authorisation from the chief accountant for the appointment and removal of all employees. Unused clock cards should be kept in a secure place by someone other than the production manager. They should be issued weekly by a responsible official.
The Payroll is not currently 'authorised' by a senior employee.	Errors could exist and these would not be detected.	The Payroll should be signed by the person preparing it and then authorised by the Assistant Accountant prior to the director signing the wages cheque. Prior to authorisation, the Assistant Accountant should carry out random checks on rates of pay, amendments, etc.
Overtime is not currently authorised.	Unauthorised and incorrect overtime payments could be made.	All overtime should be authorised by the Production Manager.
Access to the computer payroll system is not restricted.	Unauthorised amendments could be made, and access could be gained to confidential information thus breaching the Data Protection Act 1984.	Access should be controlled by regularly changed unique passwords.

Clocking in and out procedures are not supervised.	Employees could be paid for work not done if fraudulent use of clock cards occurred.	Supervision of cards and timing devices should take place.
The Production Manager pays out wages alone.	Misappropriation of cash payments could occur.	Controls could be improved by having two wages clerks paying out wages. Each employee should also sign for their wages after providing identification; no employee should be permitted to take another's wages without written authorisation.
Salary increases are not currently notified in writing.	Unauthorised increases could be made.	All increases should be notified in writing by the Chief Accountant after authorisation by a director.
Personnel records are not currently kept for administrative staff and appointments are authorised by the Finance Director.	Undetected errors could occur and inappropriate appointments could be made.	Personnel records should be kept as for production staff, and appointments and dismissals authorised by all directors.

2   Solution

Client:	**Appendex Ltd**	**W/P Ref:**	**F1/3**
Y/E Date:	**X/X/XX**		
		Prepared by:	**X**
		Date:	**X/X/XX**
		Reviewed by:	**Y**
		Date:	**X/X/XX**

WEAKNESS	EFFECT	RECOMMENDATIONS
Mr Barnes has considerable control over this system. He is responsible for ordering goods, checking goods receipts notes to his orders and invoices, as well as authorising invoices and payments to suppliers.	It is possible for Mr Barnes to defraud the company by authorising invoices for payment for which goods have not been received. These invoices could even be made out in fictitious company names made up by Mr Barnes and then paid into his bank accounts.	An appropriate segregation of duties should be set up here possibly with Mr Barnes ordering goods, a second individual checking GRNs, orders and invoices and a third authorising payments to suppliers.
Orders are confirmed by telex, with apparently no formal order document being raised.	Unauthorised orders could be placed (such as for personal use).	A formal order should be raised and signed before being sent to the supplier so both Appendex Ltd and the supplier have appropriate documentation for all orders.
The stock records appear to be updated when goods are ordered, and not when they are received. In addition, stock figures are not adjusted when deliveries occur which do not meet initial order quantities.	This will make the stock records unreliable because they will not show the actual stock levels.	The stock records should be updated from the GRN.
Invoices are not serially numbered on receipt.	Invoices could be lost during processing, causing problems with suppliers if not paid on time.	Invoices should be serially numbered on receipt.

Mr Barnes manually alters purchase invoices.	Fraudulent (undetected) amendments could be made.	Any invoices in error should be highlighted with supplies and replacement invoices requested.
No record is kept of the transfer of invoices between the accounts department and the computer department.	Invoices could be lost.	Document controls e.g., log of invoices transferred daily should be implemented.
Mr Southfork sets up new creditors ledger accounts without appropriate authority.	Invalid accounts could be set up and dummy invoices could be posted to the accounts.	An authorised individual such as Mr Barnes should authorise all new ledger accounts.
Mr Barnes decides which creditors should be paid and authorises rejections on the cheques payments listing.	This is a lack of internal control; errors could be made which would go undetected.	The cashiers office should perform this function.
The purchase ledger is only printed out once a month.	This will not show a complete audit trail if invoices are entered and paid in the same month.	A full listing of the ledger should be printed at least weekly.
A balance on a creditors listing is being used as justification to raise a cheque – this is insufficient evidence.	Payments may be made when not required or inappropriate.	When directors sign cheques they should be provided with the original invoice so they can check the validity of the payment.
Goods returns notes and credit notes are currently sent to Mr Barnes.	This results in an inadequate segregation of duties.	Goods returns notes and credit notes should be sent to the accounts department.
Supplier statements are not regularly checked to purchase ledger accounts to check for completeness and validity of entries.	Invalid or incorrect entries may be undetected.	Supplier statements should be regularly checked to purchase ledger accounts.